GOOD FRIDAY REVISITED

A TRILOGY OF ONE ACT DRAMAS SET AGAINST THE BACKDROP OF THE FIRST GOOD FRIDAY

SEAN WALSH

AT THE PRAETORIUM/
PILATE UNDER PRESSURE

VEIL

CONCLAVE

Copyright (c) 2015 by Sean Walsh

www.sean-walsh-me

DEDICATION

I dedicate this work to my good friend and mentor,
Father Martin Hogan –
without his help and encouragement
it would not have come to pass.

AT THE PRAETORIUM

If Matthew ever gets to read this script he will pause, read it again, (just to check) and then wonder how the hell Walsh got hold of his notes. He rounds out the story in Matthew's gospel, fills in the gaps, in a manner that is almost Ignatian.

Read this story, get to see it on stage someday and you will have a better understanding of what happened on that dark night in Jerusalem.

- Kevin Healy.

Pilate's dilemma is that of everyone caught between obligations to the institution one represents and loyalty to a greater truth which challenges that institution. The dramatist draws the reader/viewer into this dilemma with great skill... based on Matthew's passion narrative, in particular on elements of Matthew's passion narrative that are unique to his gospel, such as the short scene involving Pilate and his wife, the washing of hands by Pilate and the request of the Jewish authorities to place a guard on the tomb of Jesus.

Many artists have sought to gain access to the earth shattering event of the crucifixion of Jesus through various channels. These plays give us an original, imaginative and thought-provoking access... throw light on our own struggles to do what is right when it is easier to do otherwise.

- Martin Hogan.

For me, the power of the drama was in its economy of action and words, leaving the space for the audience to reach out to the message; reminiscent of Samuel Becket's chosen dramatic form.

We were presented with a weak man occupying the seat of leadership, and it hit us in the eye. He was afraid of being considered disloyal to the Roman authority, to Caesar. Afraid of the crowds, his attention was fixed submissively and fearfully on the institution and its Caesar... It couldn't be more relevant to what is happening in the Church today...

- Teresa Mee

PILATE UNDER PRESSURE

Heavily charged tension in just a few pages. Sublime economy of action and words. Powerful, convincing, elegant...

I thought it was beautifully authentic. I couldn't help thinking of all the blundering attempts of Hollywood and television screenwriters to get the tone and rhythm of antiquity – this writer nails it effortlessly!
- Sean Wiegand.

VEIL

The idea of approaching the significance of the Passion obliquely, through the experiences of those who might be regarded as enemies, is good theatre; and the actual denouement is all the more dramatic for not taking place in the presence of the Saviour.

In fact, the reality of the Incarnation seems to me properly realised in the movement – Christ's life becomes dynamic and efficacious in the world...
- Seamus Heaney.

Ingenious, totally gripping... awesome... harrowing exorcism scene... enormously stimulating...
- Mary Lappin.

CONCLAVE

Centres on a group of religious leaders, the Jewish Sanhedrin, who are so determined to preserve the status quo, from which they benefit so greatly, that they will do all in their power to eliminate anyone who threatens it.

This play, while rooted in the gospels, brings a very contemporary feel to the age old conflict between those in authority who want to protect their position and those prophetic voices who proclaim a word of truth that demands to be heard.
- Martin Hogan.

4

AT THE
PRAETORIUM
GOOD FRIDAY REVISITED

SEAN WALSH

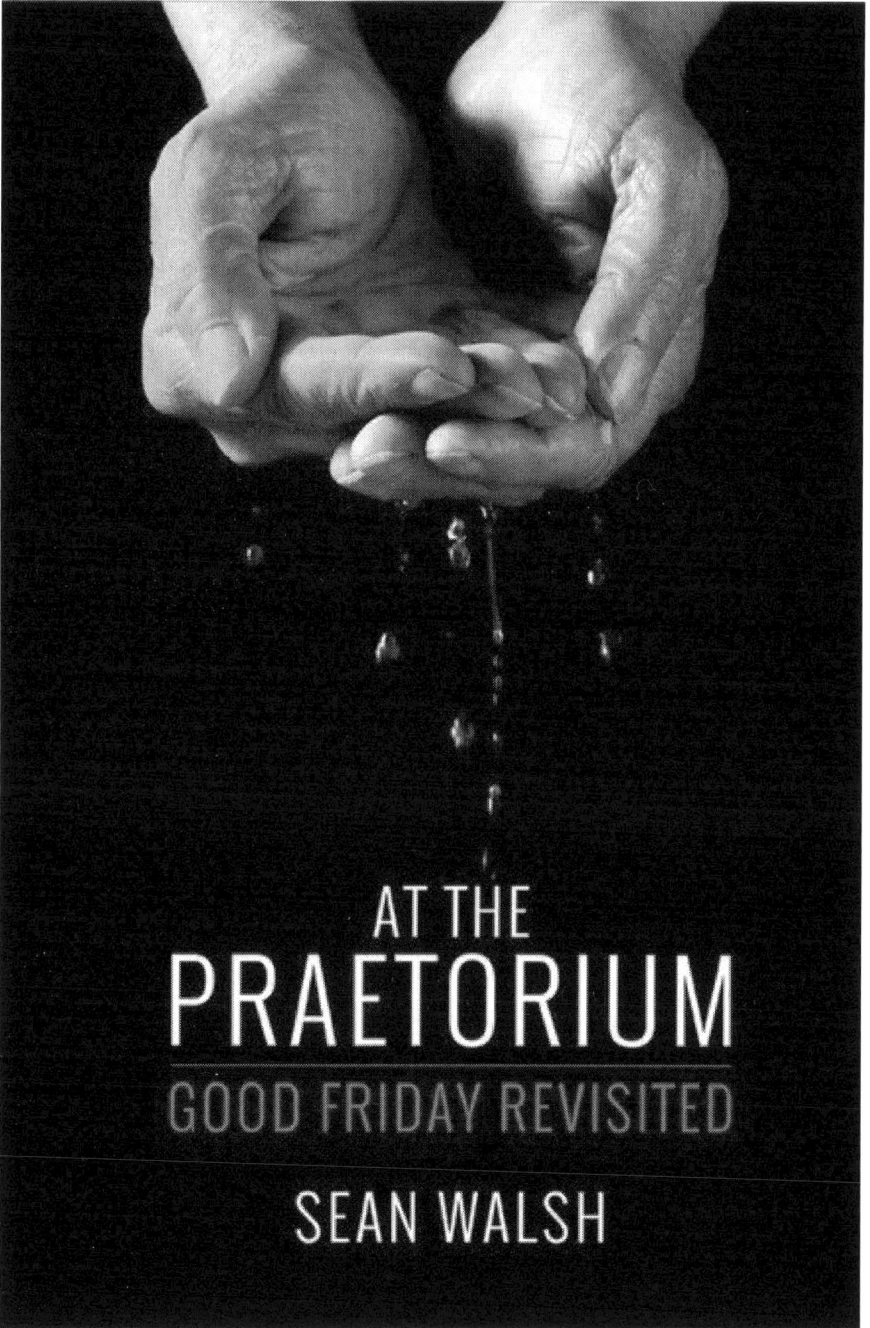

"I return to the Seat of Judgement –
have a servant fetch me water and a towel..."

NOTES

I set myself the task of telling it from the prisoners' point of view…
and as the Colonizer might have viewed it… No Jesus, no disciples,
no saints or angels, no Pharisees… 'Can be performed on a conventional stage or In the Round; in modern dress or as costume drama…

At the Praetorium… At. Above. Beneath… Behind the scenes.
Off stage… Conjecture. Irony. Dramatic license. A storyline that
could never be dismissed as incredible… 'never far from the
authenticity of the official records. What might have happened,
could well have been the case…

The piece is based, for the most part, on the Passion narrative
according to Matthew. The Evangelist does not name Pilate's wife
so I resisted giving her a fictitious one; I simply refer to her as the
Woman. (Her name was unimportant; her dream – in terms of the
ancient world – was of significant importance.)

Re the thieves who were crucified with Jesus: tradition has named
the repentant, "Dismas" and the unrepentant, "Gestas" but this is not
scriptural. In Mark's Gospel (14:32) and in Matthew's Gospel
(27:44) both are reported as berating Jesus. John's Gospel (19:18)
mentions their presence without stating that they berated Jesus.

Only in Luke's Gospel (23:39-43) is there reference to a repentant
thief; but neither are actually named.   - S W

SCENARIO

The eve of a great feast - and a great Event...

Jerusalem, the Holy City of a Chosen People, lies sleeping...

The full moon of the Passover, high in a cloudless sky, brings into cold and sharp relief the Temple... casts light and shadow on the narrow streets of the inner city....

Through these streets the elders of the Sanhedrin are hurrying to the house of Caiaphas, the High Priest...

While in the upper room of a private house the prophet from Nazareth sits down to break bread with his disciples...

In the upper city the cry of the watch rings out from the turrets of the Praetorium, the Roman fortress, symbol and sign of conquest...

Beneath the Praetorium, in the dungeons, three men lie in chains, awaiting execution:

Dismas, a thief, perhaps the greatest thief in all history - who stole Paradise even as he suffered the death penalty.

Gestas, a man who may die as he has lived.

And Jesus bar Abbas, held for murder and sedition, of whom so little is known, so much surmised - in literature and drama - even to the present day…

C A S T

BARABBAS, a prisoner

DISMAS, another

GESTAS, a third…

LUCIUS, a Roman officer.

PONTIUS PILATE.

HIS WIFE.

ZARA, her servant.

JOSEPH of ARIMATHEA.

SOLDIERS... 2/3.

SCENE ONE

LIGHT THE SET TO REVEAL A DUNGEON CELL. GESTAS AND DISMAS LIE FRONT STAGE ON STRAW, IN CHAINS.

BARABBAS LIES BACKSTAGE, ASLEEP…

GESTAS: Dismas?.. (PAUSE) 'You... you awake, Dismas?.. (PAUSE) D-D-ismas?..

DISMAS: Yes...

GESTAS: Oh. Oh, good... I... I s-s-slept a while... I - I'm cold... y'know... You sleep a while, D-Dismas?

DISMAS: Yes…

GESTAS: Eh-hh… What… what t-t-time you think it is, Dismas?..

DISMAS: Time? There is no time. Not any more. Not here. Not in this, this...

GESTAS: I know what you mean. (PAUSE) I - I had a, y'know, dream.

DISMAS: Nightmare.

GESTAS: Yeah, yes I h-h-had. You won't believe this, Dismas, but I, I -

DISMAS: Nightmare of rats and chains and stench -

GESTAS: 'Dreamt the G-G-Governor gave us a, y'know, p-p-pardon -

DISMAS: 'Not knowing the day nor the hour, season of the year...

GESTAS: What you think, D-D-Dismas? What you think of that one, huh?..

DISMAS: The winds that blow, the ships that come to our shores…

GESTAS: Pretty good, eh? Pretty good, D-D-Dismas? (PAUSE) Dismas?

DISMAS: Better to be dead.

GESTAS: Oh...

DISMAS: Yes... Yes, that was a pretty good dream…

GESTAS: Yes? You think so? 'You really –

DISMAS: Pretty... 'Ever dream about women?

GESTAS: Wh-what?

DISMAS: You know… women.

GESTAS: Oh-hh.

DISMAS: Long black hair in your face. Flashing eyes, olive skin. Her lips against yours, your heart pounding as you toss and turn, sigh and yearn - in this filthy, stinking, rotten straw!

PAUSE AFTER CRESCENDO.

GESTAS:	Eh... eh-hh...
DISMAS:	(TAUNTING) How about that, Gestas? Pretty good, eh - pretty good, Gestas?
GESTAS:	Yes. Yes, D-D-Dismas. That was -
DISMAS:	You ever dream like that, Gestas?
GESTAS:	Well no, Dismas. I mean… well, not that I - I -
DISMAS:	Welcome to the club, Gestas!
GESTAS:	Wh-what?..
DISMAS:	We are no longer men. We never will be men again.
GESTAS:	Oh… I… It never really happened, D-D-Dismas. (PAUSE) Dismas?
DISMAS:	What?
GESTAS:	That d-d-dream, Dismas. I mean, I never really dreamt that the G-G-Governor gave us a, y'know, a –
DISMAS:	It doesn't matter.
GESTAS:	It's just that... well, here, here in this p-p-place, you make things up, like. You know what I mean, Dismas? What I, I -
DISMAS:	They've done a very good job.
GESTAS:	Huh?
DISMAS:	Romans. Roman bastards...
GESTAS:	Well, I -
DISMAS:	Our captors, Gestas, our captors. I give them credit for that - they've done an excellent, oh, a very excellent job.
GESTAS:	(MISSING HIS MEANING) Oh-hh?.. Well, I suppose... I mean we were ou-ou-y'know,

outnumbered, Dismas. We really were.

DISMAS: Leaving us like this...

GESTAS: I've never seen s-s-soldiers fight like that, D-D-Dismas. You ever seen soldiers fight like that, D-Dismas?

DISMAS: Chained us to the bowels of the earth and threw away the key.

GESTAS: A ph-ph-phalanx...

DISMAS: Left us to be crushed under the weight of - what? Our own hopelessness?...

GESTAS: We just didn't know, did we, Dismas? We just didn't know.

DISMAS: Not knowing, that's what makes it so... Not even knowing whether we be really alive or dead...

GESTAS: I drew b-b-blood, y'know, before they took me. D-D-Did you know that, Dismas? Oh yes. I drew b-blood, all right. I was up, right up at the gates when they t-t-took me, y'know, p-p-prisoner...

SUDDEN SARDONIC LAUGH FROM DISMAS.

GESTAS: Wh-what?

DISMAS: Whether we be alive or dead - that's it! Don't you see, you feckless fool, we're dead! We died that day in the battle, fell in the thick of it as they forced the main gates closed against our onslaught. We were cut down and died - there in the dust and stones and

12

first heat of day!

GESTAS: Wh-what are you s-s-saying?

DISMAS: We're dead, Gestas, dead! And now we live the other life. No end to this darkness, this - not knowing. No pardon, no reprieve, no walking out in daylight, ever. Just this, without end. And that's what makes it – Hell!

GESTAS: No? No-oh! You're j-j-joking, you must be j-j-joking! No, I -

DISMAS: Right, I'm joking, right, all right!.. I'm - joking. Pull your hair, scratch your eyes, bite your tongue. Yes, we are alive.

            So hush, Gestas - there's a guard outside who takes especial delight in laying a scourge across our backs...

GESTAS: Oh, D-D-Dismas –

DISMAS: Oh, Gestas. Our jailers have done their work well.

GESTAS: Huh?

DISMAS: We're very near the edge now, Gestas, very near the edge.

            BARABBAS SIGHS, GROANS, CRIES OUT IN HIS SLEEP:

BAR: No, I... No, no – no!.. 'Can't be dead... can't... I -

PAUSE AS HIS VOICE TRAILS AWAY...

GESTAS: Bar-Bar-Barabbas again. You hear th-that?

DISMAS: Hmmm.

GESTAS: Over and over... He lives the s-s-same hour in his
           sleep day after d-d-day, night after, y'know, night. He
           is driving me -

DISMAS: Yes.

GESTAS: B-b-but it was only a caravan in a, y'know, mountain
           pass. I mean, why does he have to go over and over
           it?.. W-W-We took many a, y'know, caravan in the
           old days.

DISMAS: Oh no. There was a difference.

GESTAS: What?

DISMAS: He killed an unarmed man without mercy - that's the
           difference, Gestas. That day in the mountains... A fat,
           whimpering merchant who kissed his feet and
           begged, begged for –

GESTAS: B-b-but he was in league with the, y'know, R-R-
           Romans.

DISMAS: Was he? Anyone know for certain? Had his case been
           tried, proven?

GESTAS: Well, I –

DISMAS: Oh, Barabbas was out of sorts that day, his mind
           crazed by rumours of Roman atrocities in Jerusalem.
           He drew and killed the merchant. I've seen him kill

before but never in cold blood… If he lives to old age he will still be haunted by –

IN HIS SLEEP BARABBAS EXCLAIMS AGAIN.

GESTAS: C-c-crazy, crazy Barabbas. D-d-dreamer, damned dreamer. If only he had contented himself with r-r-robbery in-in-stead of-of –

DISMAS: Turning to revolt and rebellion.

GESTAS: And D-D-Dismas, Dismas! We f-f-followed him.

DISMAS: We always followed him. Always.

GESTAS: Oh, B-B-Barabbas, Barabbas... where you've led us... Is he..? Do you think h-h-he's near the edge, Dismas?

DISMAS: Hmmm? Oh... I –

GESTAS: Y-Yes?

DISMAS: He may just outwit the Romans in the end.

GESTAS: I, I don't...?

DISMAS: The wound in his side has begun to fester.

GESTAS: Oh-hh.

DISMAS: He's a strong man, yes, but even he... Yes, he may die before they can… press him over the –

THE CLANKING OF ARMOUR… KEYS.

DISMAS: Schhhhh...

CELL DOOR PULLED OPEN. LUCIUS ENTERS.

AT HIS SIDE, A MERCENARY…

LUCIUS: Well, well, well… Rats in their nest…

DISMAS: (IGNORING THE INTRUDER) It has a smell all its
            own - did you know that, Gestas?

GESTAS: Wh-what?

DISMAS: Fresh air. Oh, you mark my words. Fresh air has a
            smell - a sweet, sweet smell - all it's own.

LUCIUS: Stench... Give me that torch… Now go.

GUARD: But Sir -

LUCIUS: Leave me. They're chained. Besides, they're so weak
            by now... It would be like stamping on vermin... Go.

GUARD: (GOING)   Sir...

LUCIUS: Hmmmm... So who have we here?... You!.. Look at
            me!

            PAUSE. GESTAS EXCLAIMS IN PAIN.

            Ha. Does light bother you?.. Hmmm… One, two...

            LUCIUS CROSSES SLOWLY...

LUCIUS: And this, I take it, is Barabbas... king of the rabble...
            Will you speak to Lucius, king?... (PAUSE) Will

you parley with the officer of the Guard?... (PAUSE)
Speak... (PAUSE)... Speak or by Appollo I will -

DISMAS: (HASTILY) He is not well.

GESTAS: W-w-wound. Wound he got in the - the –
DISMAS: He has a fever.
LUCIUS: Hmmm… Has he, indeed?.. Then we'll cure it... on
            the morrow... that's for sure...
GESTAS: Wh-what does he me-me-mean?
BAR: He means I am to die.
LUCIUS: Ah-hh, Barabbas! So you've come back to us?
BAR: But not it would seem for long…
LUCIUS: Your friends will keep you company. It wouldn't do
            to give you centre stage, now would it?
GESTAS: Th-th-the three of us?
DISMAS: How?
LUCIUS: Naked. Above the earth. On a dung hill.
GESTAS: Cru-cru-crucified!?
DISMAS: But we are Jews! Our law pre –
LUCIUS: Your law? Your law prescribes? There is only one
            law in force in this desert land - a law called Pontius
            Pilate. That law is right now above us.
BAR: Pilate - here?
LUCIUS: 'Come with full militia from the coast to make a show
            of strength in your miserable city. The smell is in his
            nose, on his clothes. Oh, he's in wicked mood...

He returns to Caesarea at the end of the Feast.

DISMAS: Feast?

LUCIUS: Your Feast of Passover.

DISMAS: The Passover!

BAR: Then - then there is a full moon.

LUCIUS: And a dry cold that goes to the very marrow.
              Her ladyship has taken to her bed.

BAR: The city - city will be crowded. Our fellow men…
              from across the sea… from north and south and the
              lands of the farther west...

LUCIUS: (DRILY) Money-bags crowding your taverns from
              every corner of the Empire.

GESTAS: It's a th-th - y'know, thieves' paradise –

DISMAS: Where we were kings upon a time…

              LUCIUS CROSSES TO THE CELL DOOR.

LUCIUS: Business, big business. The vendors are doing a
              roaring trade... And your fathers of the Temple, the
              greybeards of prayer and penance, are grabbing for
              gold with the rest! Your cult of the gods is a shallow
              show...

DISMAS: (UNDER HIS BREATH) Bastard...

LUCIUS: You said...?

BAR: Nothing. He said - a prayer, that's all...

LUCIUS: Hmmm... Well, that's it, then. You go up with the
            sun...

            One of my men will bring you a stew by and by...
            Dine well, my rebels... Dine - and be damned!

            EXIT LUCIUS... FADE LIGHTS...
            MUSIC... FADED UP... THEN OUT...

SCENE TWO

LIGHT AREA TO ONE SIDE. BIRDSONG...
PILATE STANDS... STRETCHES... YAWNS.
ENTER LUCIUS.

LUCIUS: Good morning, Sir.

PILATE: Ah, Lucius... Up and about so early?

LUCIUS: I, I slept but fitfully, Sir.

PILATE: And I. The journey from the coast should have tired
            me. And yet I was restless through all the long hours
            of darkness. As was her ladyship...

LUCIUS: Sir, I should tell you -

PILATE: But now the sun is up, the air balmly, while the city
            still slumbers.

LUCIUS: Sir, I -

PILATE: See, Lucius. Below and about us. Jerusalem. Have
            you ever viewed a more peaceful vista?

LUCIUS: Well, no, Sir. Not, not since we departed Italy.

PILATE: Yet so much unrest down there - discontent, anger,
            railing against Rome - in the squares, the narrow
            streets, the squalid dwelling places...

LUCIUS: An unrest that is fermenting, Sir, even as we speak.

PILATE: What?

LUCIUS: The Jews are on the move, Sir. Crowds of them,
            converging here – on the Praetorium.

PILATE:	Oh?
LUCIUS:	My intelligence is they are in contentious mood. 'Roused by their religious leaders.
PILATE:	Oh, ye gods! And I in high hope of a peaceful sojourn.
LUCIUS:	It would seem unlikely, Sir.
PILATE:	Such a troublesome Race! What is it this time?
LUCIUS:	The Rabbis - priests of the Temple - have a prisoner.
PILATE:	Prisoner?
LUCIUS :	One of their own. Jesus. 'Hails from the North. From Galilee.
PILATE:	And?
LUCIUS :	They would have you try him - they are intent on obtaining the death penalty.
PILATE:	Why? What has the wretch done to warrant crucifixion?
LUCIUS:	Magic. Sorcery. Leading the people astray. Disturber of the Peace. Incitement to revolt and rebellion...
PILATE:	What? Against Rome?
LUCIUS:	'Claims to be their King.
PILATE:	King? Of the Jews? Huh...
LUCIUS:	Any moment now they will be at the gates of this fortress, clamouring for a hearing.
PILATE:	Ah, but why the urgency?
LUCIUS:	'Hard to tell with the Jews, Sir - well nigh impossible to read their minds.
PILATE:	Hmmm... Is there something here below the surface?..

Oh, very well. I will go down to them anon. Now
leave me, Lucius. See to your garrison.

LUCIUS: Sir...

EXIT LUCIUS.

PILATE: Hmmm... What is afoot here? What hidden from the
eye?
'A people apart, their ways not our ways...
Jesus, eh. Jesus... King of the Jews?.. King of the
rabble, more like...
But if he is their King why would they want him done
to death?
Well... we shall see...
Of this they can be assured:
they will have nothing from me but Roman justice –
and Roman order.
The Peace of the Empire is all.
I will not tolerate disorder, countenance disruption...
I, Pontius Pilate, Governor of Judaea by the gift of
Caesar, will maintain the Pax Romana at all costs…
all costs.

DIM LIGHTS.

SCENE THREE

THE DUNGEON... SUDDENLY GESTAS CRIES
OUT - THE CRY OF A MAN IN THE GRIP OF A
TERRIBLE FEAR. CLANKING OF CHAINS AND
PANTING AS BARABBAS STRUGGLES
ACROSS THE CELL FLOOR -

BAR: Gestas!.. Gestas!!!
GESTAS: I don't want to die... not like that... not -
BAR: Shut up!
GESTAS: Cru-cru-cruci -

BARABBAS STRIKES GESTAS ACROSS THE
FACE.

BAR: Not here, not when we are their prisoners... I could
            not bear the thought of a man of mine whimpering
            like a stray cur...
GESTAS: Barabbas, you were always kind to me, Bar -
            (BEGINNING TO BREAK AGAIN) T-t-they're
            going to nail us up, Bara –
BAR: Shut! Shut your mouth! If they hear you they
            will mock us all the more. Do you want to die like a
            man - or a slave?
GESTAS: D-d-don't want to –

BAR:	Gestas! You make another outcry like that and - I swear it, Gestas, I swear it - I'll strangle you with this chain!
GESTAS:	I won't, I p-p-promise you I -
DISMAS:	Leave him be. If - if he is afraid he is not the only one.
BAR:	What!?
DISMAS:	Yes, Barabbas. Yes! I can think of nothing else - and I am so afraid I - I can't contain my... myself.
BAR:	Now listen –
DISMAS:	You may be a man of steel but –
BAR:	Listen to me! We have come a long way together. You and Gestas and I. Now we've come to the end of the road. The dice is loaded against us. But by the God of Israel we are going to die as we have lived - as men of Israel! A few hours from now they will take us. All right, then. But I intend to die in the company of men - not sewer rats!
GESTAS:	We - we won't let you down, Barabbas –
DISMAS:	When the time comes –
BAR:	When the time comes we walk out of this Roman fortress with our heads high and a cry for Israel on our lips. Understood?
GESTAS:	Yes. Yes, B-B-B –
DISMAS:	Yes –
BAR:	All right, then... All right.

SCENE FOUR

LIGHT SECOND AREA: THE WOMAN STANDS,
HOLDING A SMALL, ORNAMENTAL DISH,
CALLING:

WOMAN: Zara?.. Zara?!..

ENTER ZARA…

ZARA: Coming, my lady... I was fetching water for your -

WOMAN: Such a commotion!

ZARA: Oh? It woke you?

WOMAN: No matter, that. I had a fretful night... So? What is it?

ZARA: Of no great import, my lady. But a crowd of Jews -

WOMAN: Crowd? More like a mob -

ZARA: Come to importune the Governor -

WOMAN :   Importune? To what purpose?

ZARA: They have brought one of their own race to him for judgment.

WOMAN: Oh?

ZARA: One Jesus of Nazareth. The rumours about him are rife -   (WOMAN TAKEN ABACK)
My Lady?

WOMAN: This Jew, this Jesus - describe him.

ZARA: Why, I cannot, my lady. His face is bruised, bloodied
-

THE WOMAN DROPS THE DISH.

            Oh, your precious dish! Broken now beyond repair...
WOMAN: No matter, that. Leave it... Zara, you will go at once
            to my husband, tell him he must have nothing to do
            with this man -
ZARA: But, but my lady -
WOMAN: I dreamt I suffered much on his account -
ZARA: The Governor is, even now, on the Seat of Judge -
WOMAN: You must get my message to him, girl! You must! It
            is of the utmost importance! Go - now!
ZARA: I, I -
WOMAN: Do it!..
ZARA: As you wish, my lady...

EXIT ZARA.

WOMAN: Bloodied... bruised... The face in my dream...

DIM LIGHTS.

SCENE FIVE

THE DUNGEON…

GESTAS: I - I don't know how to p-p-pray...

BAR: Well, isn't that just too bloody bad?..

GESTAS: I mean, what do you...? Is there s-s-someone...?
            Will… y'know, will anyone hear... it...? (PAUSE)
            I've...I've often thought about t-t-things... y'know,
            things… I think, like, a lot about... y'know, d-d-
            different things... What, what do you think,
            Barabbas?.. I mean, do you think there's... there's a
            god?..

BAR: If there is I don't know him. I don't know him at
            all.

GESTAS: Wh-what do you think, Dismas?

DISMAS: Haven't thought about it much... He's made a mess of
            it if he is - if there is a god...

BAR: (LAUGHING SARDONICALLY) Here we are,
            prisoners, in chains, spending our last day in a hole in
            the ground, and we wonder if there's a good god?!
            It's as simple as that - good god!

GESTAS: Yes, yes I see what you mean.

DISMAS: Then what happens when the time comes... when we
            go up and it's - all over?

BAR: Nothing. Just that. When you're dead, you're dead.

DISMAS: I don't know. But it can't be as you say. Just can't.

There must be some –

BAR: 'Ever met anyone who came back?.. (PAUSE) Dismas. Look, I'll tell you: the day someone comes back from the dead I'll begin to think about it - not till then.

DISMAS: If there was something I could - believe in... I remember once, when I was a boy, in the Synagogue on a Sabbath. The Rabbi told us about - the next life.

BAR: He didn't say how much was in the coffers, did he?

GESTAS: I s-s-suppose it will be like, y'know, falling asleep... only we won't ever wake up... Pain. There will be a lot of p-p-pain, at first... Oh-hh. 'Lot of pain... B-B-Blood. That's it. The blood will leave us, drain away, run down the crosses... and everything will get d-d-darker and darker... We'll get very d-d-dizzy... not dizzy-sick, just, y'know, dizzy... and then everything will go b-b-black...

BAR: And that will be that.

DISMAS: I wonder. When I was a boy I didn't have any - doubts. I wish I...

GESTAS: I suppose... imagine it's harder to watch a man die than to... y'know, die… yourself... I mean when you're w-w-watching -

BAR: Jerusalem.

GESTAS: Wh-what?

BAR: Jerusalem. It will be the last thing we'll see before – it gets darker and darker... Our city. City we fought in, fought for. Jerusalem... Some day it will be a city of freedom, as great as Rome in the eyes of men...

GESTAS: P-p-people... many people from all over the w-w-world will come here.

DISMAS: Will they remember us?

BAR: They will. Our cause is not lost. They will recall the men who died this day.

GESTAS: M-m-mebbe they will even build a, y'know, mo-mo-monument over the place where we - I mean, where we'll be p-p-put up.

BAR: You're really hanging on, aren't you?

CELL DOOR UNLOCKING... BOLTS, CHAINS...

BAR: This is it. Remember what I said - Gestas?

GESTAS: Yes, Bar -

BAR: Dismas?

DISMAS: Yes, I -

ENTER LUCIUS... FOLLOWED BY A GUARD.

BAR: Well?..

LUCIUS: There's been a delay.

DISMAS: What?

LUCIUS: You may have company. One of yours has been brought in for trial. Jesus. Jesus of Nazareth.

BAR: What's that got to do with us? I don't know the man.

LUCIUS: You may get to know him before long. Pilate is trying the case. If the Jews get their way you may all go up together.

DISMAS: The Jews?

LUCIUS: Well, they arrested him. Last night. They brought him to Pilate this morning. Right now they're demanding the death sentence.

GESTAS: Wh-wh-what's his, y'know, line - I mean, what's he done?

LUCIUS: Usurper of the peace. Claims he's king of the Jews. At least so your crowd say. I think he's some kind of religious fanatic.

GESTAS: B-b-but we don't want to die with a y'know, religious fanatic.

LUCIUS: You don't have much choice, do you?

HE MOTIONS TO THE SOLDIER.

Unlock them…

THE SOLDIER FREES THEM, MOVING IN TURN FROM ONE TO ANOTHER… MEANWHILE:

DISMAS: Wh-What..?

LUCIUS: A small gesture, nothing more... We'll just have to
             wait and see. I'll bring you word... Meanwhile I've
             brought you something for your pains.

HE HANDS THEM A FLASK...

DISMAS: Wine? Is it?
GESTAS: Oh-hh! I - I haven't had a drink for –
BAR: Our thanks for this.
LUCIUS: For nothing. As I say, it's for your pains... You will
             have pain, that's for sure... When I come again it will
             be for the last time... I will be coming for you...

LUCIUS AND THE SOLDIER EXEUNT...

THE PRISONERS FALL ON THE WINE, AD-
LIBBING... BARABBAS DISPENSES...

BAR: God of Israel!
DISMAS: Some for me, Barabbas! Oh, where's my cup?
GESTAS: An'- an'- and me! Fair deal, huh?.. Y'know...
             Remember, member the old days, Ba-Ba-Barabbas!..
             Equal shares for all... I mean fair is –
BAR: And we can drink unfettered - drink unfettered!
DISMAS: I've found it - here!
GESTAS: (ATTEMPTING TO STAND) Can't... can't stand...
             y'know?.. I hope the wine - ha, ha, ha - wine isn't as

	weak as my knees!
DISMAS:	Hmmm. It's a good wine.
GESTAS:	Yes, yes! Bloody good wine!
DISMAS:	You haven't tasted it yet.
GESTAS:	Well, I... I mean any, any wine would be b-b-bloody good wine this m-m-minute, y'know...
BAR:	More, Dismas? Don't gulp, Gestas.
GESTAS:	No, Barabbas. Indeed I won't... gulp, Barabbas... (PAUSE...) Here, why... Barabbas, why don't we drink a, y'know, t-t-toast?
DISMAS:	Yes! Yes, good idea, Gestas. Why don't we just do that?..
BAR:	All right, then... All right. More for you, Gestas... Dismas... Now let me see. (PAUSE)… I know.
GESTAS:	Y'know...
BAR:	Gentlemen, I give you a toast - to Jesus of Nazareth! Our fellow fanatic!..
GESTAS:	Albeit a r-r-religious one.
DISMAS:	May his trial go smoothly –
GESTAS:	H-h-have a happy ending –
BAR:	And may all the sons of men be content –
DISMAS:	Forever and ever –
ALL 3:	Amen...

THEY TOUCH MUGS... LIGHTS FADE...

SCENE SIX

LIGHT AN AREA TO ONE SIDE.
ENTER PILATE AND LUCIUS.

PILATE: Yes, Lucius, what is it?

LUCIUS: Sir, your wife sends an urgent warning -

PILATE: Warning?

LUCIUS: You are to have nothing to do with this man. Last
            night she dreamt she suffered much on his account.

PILATE: She said that? You are certain?

LUCIUS: Just now. Her slave, Zara, came directly to -

PILATE: Oh-hh... None of this is to my liking.

LUCIUS: Can it be a sign, portent?..

PILATE :   What to make of it? I am astounded at this Jesus. He
            speaks not a word in his own defence. Why, he will
            not even look at me. 'Stands there, centre-circle,
            downcast...

LUCIUS: The Jews bear him much malice.

PILATE: They are bent on blood. But why? Why the hatred?

LUCIUS: And they are playing the Roman card.

PILATE: Huh... I am loath to give in to them. And yet the more
            I try the more unruly they become.

LUCIUS: Eh, if I may remind you, Sir -

PILATE: What?

LUCIUS: It is the custom at the Feast for the Governor to release to the people a prisoner of their choice.

PILATE: Yes. Yes, of -

LUCIUS: There are many felons in the dungeons. I have in mind one in particular -

PILATE: Who? Tell me -

LUCIUS: Jesus. Son of Abbas.

PILATE: Barabbas. He still lives? I found him guilty of sedition and murder. A vile creature.

LUCIUS: He is to be executed this very day. With two others.

PILATE: Come! To the point!

LUCIUS: Well, if you were to offer to release one or the other – Barabbas or the Galilean?

PILATE: Ah! I see what you - !

LUCIUS: We will foil the Rabbis, slip their snare -

PILATE: But of course! No one could be so malevolent as to prefer a murderer to a mute!.. I thank you, Lucius... Come, let us return to the Seat of Judgement!

EXEUNT PILATE AND LUCIUS. FADE LIGHTS.
CROWD TUMULT, OFF... AND FADE.

SCENE SEVEN

LIGHT ROOM, AS BEFORE. THE WOMAN
PACING... ENTER ZARA.

WOMAN: Well? Did you..?

ZARA: Indeed, my lady. I went at once to the Place of
           Judgment as you bade me, gave your message to one
           of the guards who went directly to the Centurion -

WOMAN: And he conveyed as much to my husband?

ZARA: Be assured of it. Word for word.

WOMAN: Oh-hh. Then we can only wait and... And still the
           tumult grows apace.

ZARA: It frightens me, my lady. The crowds are in a frenzy,
           at fever pitch.

WOMAN: Oh, how will it go for the Jew - and for my husband?

ZARA: I have seen many prisoners come and go – witnessed
           their trials at a distance - but this, this...

WOMAN: Yes?..

ZARA: Why, he stands alone before the Procurator, this Jesus
           of Nazareth. Not one of his own Race lifting a finger -
           much less a voice - in his defence. Whatever friends
           he had - family, following - have all deserted him...

FADE LIGHTS ON WOMAN AND ZARA.
CROWD TUMULT, OFF... AND FADE.

SCENE EIGHT

LIGHT PILATE AND LUCIUS, ENTERING.

PILATE: Oh, ye gods! Am I to believe my ears?! How cold! How sinisterly callous! That they should choose Barabbas, call for his release, scream instead for the execution of one in whom I can find no malice!..

LUCIUS: These people are not to blame, Sir - not the Jews.

PILATE: What?

LUCIUS: This is the work of the Sanhedrin.
The Rabbis have moved among the crowds,
egging them on, whipping them into a frenzy,
spurring them to call for the release of Barabbas.

PILATE: Yes. Yes, well be it so, I still –

LUCIUS: Sir, I am your commanding officer, a centurion of the Empire. I think as a military man, not as a politician. And the warrior in me says there is a mob at our gates, that this garrison fortress of ours is under siege.

PILATE: So?

LUCIUS: I have a full company of militia on stand-by, at high alert. And I have positioned archers on the rooftop, at the turrets. You have but to nod, Procurator, and I will disperse this mob, lift this siege...

PILATE: Ah, but there would be bloodshed, Lucius - almost certainly - and where would it end, once begun?.. Are we to make martyrs of these fanatics?

Might not an uprising spread throughout this accursed

country, precipitated at our gates?..

And once word reached Rome - as it most certainly

would - how should it rebound on me?..

No. No, there is another way.

LUCIUS: Sir?

PILATE: I return to the Seat of Judgment. Have a servant

fetch me water and a towel.

LUCIUS: (TAKEN ABACK) But, Sir, I - ?!..

PILATE: Do it. And at once!

LUCIUS: Sir…

EXIT LUCIUS

PILATE: I will disperse this mob, lift this siege. In my own

way. And without bloodshed...

ANGRY TUMULT, OFF-STAGE... FADE...

SCENE NINE

LIGHT THE DUNGEON.

DISMAS: Empty. Every last drop - gone…

GESTAS: We'll all be empty s-s-soon. Y'know, empty.

BARABBAS TALKS ALOUD IN HIS SLEEP…

BAR: Caravan…

GESTAS: Huh?!

BAR: (EXCLAIMING) Take him! Him and all his
            following!.. This fat bastard grovels to the Romans -
            then why should he live longer? He has whored with
            the pagans, then let him die!

DISMAS: Now for blood.

GESTAS: Wh-what?

DISMAS: Hush...

BAR: So…? You crawl on your belly and beg for mercy?..
            No! No, you die! – Now!.. Ah-hhhh-hhh!..

A DISTRAUGHT BARABBAS:

            O-o-ohhh... Is he dead? Dead, Dismas?.. O-oh-hhh...

GESTAS: We'll all be dead s-s-soon –

DISMAS: Hold your tongue!

BAR: (COMING TO)

            Is he dead? Dismas?.. Dismas, is he dead?... His
            blood is on my hands, Dismas, on my hands…

DISMAS: Wine, Barabbas. Wine.

BAR: What?..

DISMAS: We've all had a fair share of wine - the wine
            Lucius gave us...

BAR: Oh... Oh, yes... Just what did he put in that flask?..
            Roman swine...

DISMAS: It was a good wine, Barabbas. We've got to grant him
            that.

GESTAS: B-b-bloody great wine if, if you ask me.

BAR: Nobody asked.

GESTAS: Well, I mean –

BAR: Nobody cares... Nobody cares what you mean,
            Gestas. Not anymore. Not now... So it was a good
            wine? So it was a bad wine? So we drank it, no?..

GESTAS: Yes. Yes, Barabbas. T-t-that's for sure.

BAR: Good or bad we drank it… All right, then. We drank it. What's done is done. Finished. Good or bad, down the drain... Down the cross… Red wine running down the cross... like blood… draining away… like bloody good wine…

Dizzy... not dizzy sick - y'know - just dizzy... And Jersualem going up and over and round... round an' round... round and round!.. Oh what did that Roman put in the wine?..

FADE LIGHTS…

ANGRY MOB, OFF. AND FADE…

SCENE TEN

LIGHT ROOM. THE WOMAN AND ZARA.

POINT, COUNTERPOINT:

ZARA: And the Centurion came upon me where I was
          standing to one side -
WOMAN: Oh, what is he about, my husband? -
ZARA: 'Bade me fetch a basin of water and a towel -
WOMAN: Disregards my counsel, declines my advice, ignores
          my admonition -
ZARA: Hurry back to him -
WOMAN: Wash his hands, wash his hands -
ZARA: And so I did -
WOMAN: In full view, full view! -
ZARA: And he in turn -
WOMAN: Cleansing himself of guilt, of ignominy?!.

THEY TURN TO EACH OTHER AGAIN.

ZARA: My lady?
WOMAN: Ah, but in the days and nights and years to come -
          when he is far from pomp and ceremony, relieved of
          office - how will he salve his conscience?..

DARKEN THE WOMAN AND ZARA.

SCENE ELEVEN

LIGHT PILATE AND LUCIUS.

PILATE: Lucius.

LUCIUS: Sir?

PILATE: Release Barabbas. He walks - if he can walk - free.

LUCIUS: Sir. And the Galilean?

PILATE: Have him scourged. Let your militia have their way
            with him a while.

LUCIUS: As you wish. And then?..

PILATE: Then… if the Jews do not relent... If, if they continue
            to bay for blood...

LUCIUS: Sir?

PILATE: Crucify him.

DARKEN PILATE AND LUCIUS.
ANGRY CROWD, OFF, AS BEFORE... AND
FADE.

SCENE TWELVE

LIGHT THE WOMAN.

WOMAN: Jesus... Jesus of Nazareth...

          What manner of man is this that he will not speak

          as much as a word in his own defence?..

          Does he not realise how dangerous is his very

          silence?..

          Can it be that he is unaware of my husband's power -

          to grant his life or condemn him to death?..

          As if - as if he was resigned to die -

          could that be the sum of it?..

ENTER ZARA.

ZARA: It is bad, my lady.

WOMAN: How bad?

ZARA: The word has gone out from the Seat of Judgement.

          The prisoner has been led away.

          The soldiers are to scourge him -

WOMAN: Scourged!.. That it should come to this.

          Oh, I have seen felons after scourging.

          Bloodied, raw, flesh torn from the very bone...

          What has he done, this just man,

          to merit whipping by a demented militia?..

ZARA:	You must not fret so, my lady.
	Else you will come down with a -
WOMAN:	Zara...
ZARA:	My lady?
WOMAN:	You will follow them at a safe distance, witness by
stealth	what you can...
ZARA:	But, but, my lady -
WOMAN:	Go. Do it, Zara.
ZARA:	Oh, I, I -
WOMAN:	For my sake, girl. And yours.
ZARA:	Well, my lady. Very well... I can only try...

DARKEN SET AS ZARA MAKES TO LEAVE.

SCENE THIRTEEN

THE DUNGEON… AS BEFORE.

GESTAS: I, I t-t-think I feel… bit dizzy... not just dizzy - dizzy
            sick... y'know?..

DISMAS: You going to throw up?

GESTAS: Oh, no! No, Dismas! No, I just –

BAR: So we're drunk… So we drank a bottle of bloody
            good wine - or a bottle of something that tasted like
            bloody good wine, looked like bloody good wine... So
            we're drunk! That doesn't mean we don't know what
            we're saying...?

GESTAS: No, of course n-n-

BAR: Doesn't mean we don't know what's going on?

GESTAS: Well! We know well wh-wh-what's going on,
            Barabbas.

BAR: What's going on - tell us?..

GESTAS: Well, I mean… we're u-u-up against it, aren't we?

BAR:	So we got drunk... When you're up against it and you can't see a way out, get drunk... When you don't know the answers, get drunk... When the world has come to a full stop and you want to convince yourself that it's still going round and round, get drunk... When they're going to crucify you, get drunk... You won't feel so badly... won't hold it against them...

BARABBAS BEGINS TO LAUGH MIRTH-
LESSLY, DISMAS AND GESTAS JOIN IN,
NERVOUSLY.

HE STOPS ABRUPTLY. PAUSE.

BAR:	Dismas... Dismas, this son of a bitch is feeling sick. Not just dizzy sick but, y'know, real sick. Any moment now, Dismas, any moment this son of a bitch is liable to throw up -
GESTAS:	Why no, Barabbas. No, I -
BAR:	Throw up, Dismas! Throw up in this, the royal suite of the House of Israel –
GESTAS:	B-B-Barabbas, I -
BAR:	What do you think of that, Dismas? Eh-hh?
DISMAS:	Well, I think it's going a bit far -
BAR:	Far? You think a bit - you think it's going a bit far? It's going a bit bloody too far, I'll tell you...

No, Dismas, no! This son of a bitch has gone too far. Not just dizzy sick – sick! Far too far.

GESTAS: (PROTESTING) Wh-wh-what? Barabbas, I m-m-mean –

BAR: On your feet, you. No one throws up in the royal suite.

BARABBAS LAYS HOLD OF GESTAS.

GESTAS: No wait! Wh-wh-what? I don't - !

BAR: Sentence has been passed! Dismas, hold the prisoner.

GESTAS: Bar-bar!.. Dismas! I s-s-swear I'm not -

BAR: Quiet!.. It is the decision of this court that you be taken forthwith to an opportune place and there crucified like the son of a bitch you are until such time as you bleed to bloodywell death..

GESTAS: You're j-j-joking, of course –

BAR: Against the wall, Dismas –

DISMAS: I have him –

GESTAS: No wait! Barabbas, Dismas! Wh-wh-what are you doing? Let me go! P-p-please let me –

THE THREE SWAY ACROSS THE FLOOR TO THE "FRONT WALL", GESTAS PROTESTING.

BAR: There. Now. Stretch out his arm, Dismas, hard against
            the wall. I'll see to this one.

GESTAS: Wh-wh-what are you - ?

BAR: Careful now. Make sure your nail goes through his
            wrist. You hear me, Dismas?

DISMAS: Ready when you are.

BAR: All right then… Steady now. Steady. Take aim and -

            BARABBAS AND DISMAS MIME HAMMERING
            AS THEY EXCLAIM:

            Bang!
            Bahm!
            Bang!
            Bahm!
            Bang!
            Bahm!
            Bang!
            Bahm!

            THEY STOP… SWAYING ON THEIR FEET…
            BREATHLESS.

GESTAS STANDS, ARMS OUTSTRETCHED, HIS
BACK TO THE AUDIENCE.

BAR: There, that should do it. We've nailed the son of a
            bitch.
DISMAS: Nice. Nice clean job.
BAR: Well, how do you feel now - friend?
GESTAS: I f-f-feel... sick.

                            LAUGHTER, JEERING.

BAR: He feels sick!
DISMAS: No, not sick – dizzy!
BAR: Not dizzy – sick!
DISMAS: Dizzy sick!
BAR: Sick dizzy!

            GESTAS MAKES TO LOWER HIS ARMS.

GESTAS: I don't like this g-g-game....

BAR: Oh no, you don't! Oh no! Keep those arms out!

DISMAS: When you're nailed, you're nailed.

BAR: Though mind you, Dismas - and I've been in this
            business a long time - they're not making nails
            anymore the way they used!

GESTAS: Never felt so d-d-dizzy...

MOCKERY

BAR: Ha! He's never been so dizzy! Never been so sick
            dizzy!

DISMAS: He's a sickener, that's what he is - the greatest
            sickener of them all! King Dizzy!

BAR: Yes, yes! Down on your knees, Dismas! Bow to the
            King of the Dizzy Sickeners!

THEY BOW THE KNEE TO GESTAS.

DISMAS: Yes, yes! All hail, King Dizzy!
BAR: Hail, Great Lord Throw Up!
DISMAS: All praise to King Dizzy!
GESTAS: I - I.... Barabbas, I...

GESTAS TURNS UPSTAGE OF A SUDDEN AND
VOMITS IN A CELL CORNER. THIS IS
GREETED WITH FURTHER LAUGHTER... AD-
LIBBING MOCKERY... DYING OUT...

BARABBAS SUDDENLY TENSES:

BAR: What was that?

DISMAS: What?

BAR: Ssssshhhh… Quiet.

            BARABBAS MOVES/CRAWLS ACROSS THE
            FLOOR, SITS WITH "HIS EAR TO A WALL…"

BAR: I thought I heard…

DISMAS: What?..

BAR: 'Sounds… like… revelry…

DISMAS: Revelry?! Down here?! Revelry!.. Oh, Barabbas!

            DISMAS BEGINS TO LAUGH… BARABBAS
            TURNS TOWARDS HIM, JOINS IN… FADE.

SCENE FOURTEEN

LIGHT THE WOMAN, PACING... ENTER
ZARA...

WOMAN: Ah, Zara. Did you?..

ZARA: As near as I dared, my lady. Oh, I am trembling.

WOMAN: What?.. Tell me.

ZARA: The mercenaries tied him to a pillar, scourged him.

WOMAN: Oh-hh. Oh, Zara.

ZARA: Then they fell to mockery - arrayed him in a scarlet
            gown.

WOMAN: Scarlet?

ZARA: For a fool.

WOMAN: Oh...

ZARA: One of them fashioned a crown of thorns, pressed it
            down on his head.

WOMAN: What?

ZARA: Another put a reed in his hand -

WOMAN: Reed?.. Ah, in place of a sceptre.

ZARA :   They took to bowing the knee, hailing him King of
            the Jews.

WOMAN: Oh, enough!

ZARA: They spat on him, struck him with the reed - jeered,
            derided him -

WOMAN: No more! Zara, no more!

ZARA:	Now they lead him back up into the sun. The Jews will again have sight of him.
WOMAN:	Oh-hh... And so he - he will be released?
ZARA:	Well, no, my lady.
WOMAN:	No?
ZARA:	If, if they persist in their demand he is to be taken out to, to -
WOMAN:	Golgotha... the place of the skull.
ZARA:	That, that is the judgment.
WOMAN:	Handed down by my husband... Oh, Pontius! Pontius Pilate! This has come between us! We two can never be as one again...

ANGRY CROWD, OFF... AND FADE.

SCENE FIFTEEN

THE DUNGEON, AS BEFORE…

BAR: I wonder what's keeping him…

DISMAS: Who?

BAR: Lucius. He said he… What's going on?.. I mean

            surely it isn't taking all this time to try a, a

            religious fanatic?

DISMAS: Mmmm… Pilate may be enjoying himself.

BAR: What?

DISMAS: Well, with Jesus. He does tricks…

BAR: Tricks?

DISMAS: Some pretty good ones – so I've heard.

            BARABBAS SNORTS AT THIS… GESTAS

            APPROACHES, SUDDENLY CURIOUS…

DISMAS: And he can tell the future.

BAR: Can he tell what will happen if the dice is loaded

            against him?

GESTAS: Wh-wh-what kind of tricks… can he do,

            Dismas?

DISMAS: Oh-hh… Like producing a coin from the mouth

of a fish or…

GESTAS: Yes?.. T-T-Tell me.

DISMAS: Changing water into wine.

BAR: And the moon is made of cheese…

DISMAS: Then there was the big one, the big trick.

GESTAS: Oh-hh?

DISMAS: Well, it was in the desert. Quite a crowd had followed him into it - into the desert. And they didn't have any food - just five loaves, that was all.

BAR: So he took the loaves and made them double and treble - and everyone had bread in plenty!

DISMAS: Yes, that, that's about right.

BAR: Dismas, I thought I knew you...

DISMAS: Well, I'm only telling you –

BAR: What you saw? Saw with your own eyes?

DISMAS: Well, no. Y'see, I met a man –

DISMAS: Who met a man who met a man. Who was a second cousin of a man who met a man who met a man...

DISMAS: That's not quite –

BAR: Ah, come off it, Dismas!

GESTAS: Yes, yes I think you ought to c-c-come off it, Dismas.

THE CELL DOOR IS UNLOCKED... BOLTS, CHAINS.

BAR: This is where we all come off it – off the ground...

THE CELL DOOR SWINGS OPEN. LUCIUS ENTERS, TWO OR THREE SOLDIERS IN ATTENDANCE.

BAR: (IN MOCK BRAVADO) Soldiers, Lucius? Are you afraid we might have recovered our strength?..

LUCIUS: You go free...

BAR: What?!

LUCIUS: You're free, understand? You walk out of here a free man.

BAR: No. No, I don't understand. Not at all.

LUCIUS: It's the custom, isn't it? To release a prisoner at the Feast?

BAR: Yes, but –

LUCIUS: Well, you're the popular choice. One man shouted your name, then a dozen, then a hundred...

GESTAS: Oh you f-f-fortunate –

DISMAS: What about the other one?

LUCIUS: Jesus? He's for Golgotha.

DISMAS: The people - did the people not ask for his
            release?

LUCIUS: On your feet. I've got work to do.

BAR: You were there, at the trial?

LUCIUS: Look, if you must know, Pilate could find little
            against the Nazarene. He wanted to release him
            but the mob started shouting for, for...

BAR: Barabbas. I see.

LUCIUS: 'Glad someone sees... All right, take these two.

            THE SOLDIERS CONVERGE ON DISMAS
            AND GESTAS.

GESTAS: (PROTESTING AS HE IS LED AWAY) But I - I
            want to die with Barabbas! I don't want to die
            with Jesus!

SOLDIER: Come on, move!

GESTAS: No, no wait! It can't be like t-t-this! There must
            be s-s-some mistake!

            GESTAS NOW FRANTIC:

Barabbas, don't let it end like this! Barabbas, I need you! Help, help me, Barabbas!.. Bar - abb - as!..

GESTAS AD-LIBBING AS HE IS DRAGGED OFF... PAUSE.

DISMAS: You know, I had this feeling all along - that you would outwit the Romans in the end.

BAR: Dismas, I –

DISMAS: Goodbye, Barabbas... Remember me.

EXIT DISMAS, FOLLOWED BY A SOLDIER.

BAR: I - I lived with them, fought with them... I had thought to die with them, never thought otherwise...

LUCIUS: Come, I'll see you to the main gates...

BAR: Dismas was my very best friend.

LUCIUS: I've got to hurry.

BAR: Yes... Yes, of course. You've got to hurry... or you'll be late... late for the stripping and the nailing...

LUCIUS: The sunlight will be strong when we get to the –

you understand?

BAR: Yes... For weeks I rotted in this Hell hole. And now I'm - it's like a dream.

LUCIUS: No dream, Barabbas, no dream... Take care, man. Go a civil way. Kill your dreams of revolt and rebellion. Kill them now, once for all. Don't end again in prison.

BAR: No... Never again. You may be sure of that.... I don't want to see the inside of a prison... ever again....

LUCIUS: Defying Rome is a fool's game....

BAR: Fool's... game...

LUCIUS: It won't always win a fool's pardon.

BAR: Fool's... pardon...

LUCIUS: Where will you go?

BAR: Go?.. Why, to Golgotha... I go to - Golgotha... I will stay to the end... as near to Dismas and Gestas as I can –

LUCIUS: You'll be near the crosses. I'll see to it.

BAR: Until it gets - darker and darker... Besides, I...

LUCIUS: Yes?

BAR: I want to look on the man who dies in my place...

FADE LIGHTS

SCENE SIXTEEN

LIGHT A SPACE TO REVEAL THE WOMAN.
SHE TURNS TO SEE PILATE, CROSSING.
HE SEES HER OF A SUDDEN... STOPS.

PILATE: You... you heard?

WOMAN: How could I not?

PILATE: I, I did what was best...

WOMAN: Oh? For whom?

PILATE: You do not understand -

WOMAN: I understand an innocent man goes to his death with
            my husband's seal of office on the warrant!

PILATE: Very well, I... I conceded. But do you not see? Had I
            resisted, there could well have been a riot, damage to
            property and people, my militia harassed, intimidated
            – even loss of life.

WOMAN: Loss of life?..

PILATE: This way, order is maintained. The crowds will
            disperse by and by. All will be as it was...

WOMAN: Yes?

PILATE: We will be able to sleep in peace in our beds – in this
            forgotten outpost, this benighted Province...

WOMAN: In - peace?

PILATE: Oh, how can I?! These are complicated issues –
            politics of the highest order, diplomacy of a most

	subtle degree! You will see, see in time that I -
WOMAN:	Is this really my husband who speaks to me thus?..
PILATE:	I did what was in the best interests of Caesar!..
WOMAN :	But of course. Caesar first. First and foremost.
PILATE :	What! A choice between the Emperor of Rome and the King of the Jews? Don't be absurd! The decision was obvious - no contention!..
WOMAN:	Oh, Pontius, Pontius! I fear for you...
PILATE:	Woman?
WOMAN:	Your judgment against the Jew may well be your undoing...

DARKEN PILATE AND WOMAN.

SCENE SEVENTEEN

THE WOMAN ALONE. SHE DOES NOT
NOTICE AS ZARA ENTERS, APPROACHES...

ZARA: My Lady?.. So forlorn?..

WOMAN: Ah, Zara... I was a long way away... What now?

ZARA: They have started out for Calvary, my lady.

WOMAN: Oh-hh...

ZARA: So weak is the Jew, he fell under the weight of the crossbeam.

WOMAN: They are making him carry it?

ZARA: No more. The Centurion singled out a foreigner in the crowd, forced him to the task.

WOMAN: Foreigner?

ZARA: He is darker than the Jews.

WOMAN: Black?

ZARA: Indeed, my lady. A visitor, perhaps, passing through Jerusalem -

WOMAN: And now he goes to Calvary, shouldering a crossbeam -

ZARA: Albeit reluctantly.

WOMAN: Strange. Strangers...

ZARA: My lady?

WOMAN: Is it not strange, Zara, that the only ones who helped - tried to help - the Galilean are strangers to these shores?

My husband - at least at first.

The Centurion.

I, in my own way.

You, after a fashion.

And now a black man, out of Africa...

ZARA: I fail to follow, my lady?

WOMAN: Each with one thing in common: we are, all of us, non believers - pagans...

DARKEN THE SET.

SCENE EIGHTEEN

FX: THUNDER, LIGHTNING… STORM… SET
IN DARKNESS. GRADUALLY LIGHT SET AS
THE STORM DIES AWAY TO REVEAL PILATE,
STANDING, FRONT STAGE.

THE WOMAN ENTERS, APPROACHES…

WOMAN: Pontius?.. Pontius?..

PILATE: Hmmm?.. What?.. Sorry, I...

WOMAN: Shall I have a servant fetch another taper?

PILATE: No. No need... The storm has abated, the light comes
           again into the sky, the sun re-appears...
           But what to make of it? And how will our astrologers
           in Rome respond when I send them my report, bye
           and bye?..
           Thunder and lightning...
           Darkness over Jerusalem at midday - midday!
           What does it mean?..

WOMAN: It means he is dead.

PILATE: What?

WOMAN: Your expendable Jew. The one in whom you could
           find no malice -

PILATE: Enough! -

WOMAN: The man you washed your hands of, sacrificed to the
            Sanhedrin as an appeasement -
PILATE: No more, I say - !
WOMAN: I warned you -
PILATE: And I warn you, woman, not to tamper further in my
            affairs of State!..
            Now go! Leave me! You know not what you say.

            ENTER LUCIUS AT THE OPPOSITE SIDE...

WOMAN: No? Then am I wrong - so very wrong - in thinking
            that my husband gave in - caved in - to mob rule?..

            PILATE, FURIOUS, MAKES TO RESPOND -
            WHEN HE CATCHES SIGHT OF LUCIUS:

PILATE: Yes, Lucius? What is it?
LUCIUS: Sir, there is a man down in the courtyard who seeks
            an audience, urgently.
PILATE: Man? What man?
LUCIUS: He hails from Arimathea. By name, Joseph.
PILATE: Did he give cause for his request?
LUCIUS: Only that he has come in haste from Golgotha – and
            that he will detain you but briefly.
PILATE: Hmmm... From Golgotha. A Jew?
LUCIUS: A man of means, my Lord - from what I could
            ascertain.

PILATE: Huh. One of them, no doubt. A follower of the -

WOMAN: See him, Pontius, I pray you. This day is not yet over.

PILATE: (RELUCTANT) Ah-hh...

WOMAN: Oh, please, my husband...

PILATE: Hmmm... My bodyguard is at hand?

LUCIUS: In the corridor and at your bidding, Sir.

PILATE :   Oh, very well... I will give ear to this Joseph of
             Arimathea...

DARKEN AREA.

SCENE NINTEEN

LIGHT AREA TO ONE SIDE TO REVEAL
JOSEPH. LIGHT ELEVATED AREA TO REVEAL
PILATE STANDING, OBSERVING JOSEPH.

PILATE: Yes?..

JOSEPH: (STARTLED, TURNING) My, my name is Jo -

PILATE: I know who you are. Come, be brief.

JOSEPH: I, I ask permission to take possession of the
             Nazarene's body.

PILATE: He is dead? You are certain?

JOSEPH:	I was there, by the cross, when he yielded up his spirit.
PILATE:	Hmmm... You were one of his followers?
JOSEPH:	A silent one, alas.
PILATE:	Huh... And what have you in mind should I grant your request?
JOSEPH:	Why, to give him a decent burial.
PILATE:	Oh?..
JOSEPH:	Out beyond Golgotha I have had a new grave fashioned from the very rock -
PILATE:	Yes?
JOSEPH:	In, in anticipation of my own burial.
PILATE:	Indeed.
JOSEPH:	There I shall lay Jesus in a clean winding sheet - with your permission.
PILATE:	And you will seal this tomb?
JOSEPH:	There is, sir, a great rock hard by the entrance. I shall have it rolled into place once the body is -
PILATE:	Then do it - with my blessing.
JOSEPH:	I thank you, Governor.
PILATE:	And that will be the end of it...

PILATE MAKES TO TURN AWAY...

JOSEPH:	Perhaps... Perhaps not.

PILATE STOPS, PAUSES, TURNS BACK...

PILATE:	What?
JOSEPH:	While he lived, sir, Jesus predicted this day - his betrayal, trial, crucifixion.
PILATE:	Hmmm -
JOSEPH:	He also foretold his resurrection.
PILATE:	His - what?
JOSEPH:	He assured us that within three days he would rise again - from the dead...
PILATE:	Are you mad? Demented?.. You seem balanced.
JOSEPH:	That was his prophesy, Sir.
PILATE:	Oh, what is it about the Jews? Why can they never leave it be - be as we are?!
JOSEPH:	Sir, I am merely recounting what his followers heard from his lips, will readily vouch for -
PILATE:	This is preposterous!
	Look you! Jo-Joseph of Arimathea!
	Mark well my words:
	no one, no one - no slave, no free man -
	no Prince, no pauper,
	no King, Monarch, Emperor,
	no mortal man or woman
	of whatever race, colour, creed
	has ever, ever, come back from the dead!
JOSEPH:	Sir, I -
PILATE:	Yet you have the audacity - the sheer gall -
	to stand there in the fading light of day
	and assert that a Jew - a mere Jew -

a Jew rejected and reviled by his own blood -

a crucified Jew, to boot -

that this, this creature - what remains of him -

will come forth anon from the grave?!..

Oh, ye Gods!...

JOSEPH: Indeed, Procurator, I -

PILATE: Enough of nonsense! You vex me further at your

peril!..

Now go! See to this, this cadaver.

I rule the living - not the dead!..

PILATE TURNS, EXITS.

JOSEPH SHRUGS, TURNS AWAY... FADE.

SCENE TWENTY

LIGHT AREA TO ONE SIDE. PILATE SEATED,
DEEP IN THOUGHT… ENTER LUCIUS.

LUCIUS: Sir?.. (APPROACHING) Sir!..

PILATE STIRS HIMSELF.

PILATE: Hmmm?.. What?

LUCIUS: There is a delegation in the forecourt.

PILATE: Delegation?

LUCIUS: Jews… They request a hearing.

PILATE: Request denied.

LUCIUS: Sir?

PILATE: I have had enough of Jews and Jewry for one day.

LUCIUS: As you wish, Sir.

LUCIUS MAKES TO EXIT.

PILATE: Eh-hhhh?..

LUCIUS: Sir?..

PILATE: Did they… signal their intent?

LUCIUS;   They - they would have you mount a guard.

PILATE: What?

LUCIUS: At the tomb… where the felon's body is buried.

PILATE STANDS UP, NOW AGAIN ALERT.

PILATE: Do I hear you aright?

LUCIUS: They are concerned, Sir, that –

PILATE: They want me to mount a guard? Send Roman mercenaries to guard a tomb? A tomb?!

LUCIUS: From what I could gather, yes.

PILATE: Are they mad? Why, I would be the laughing stock of the Empire!

LUCIUS: It seems, sir, while he still lived, this fellow promised his followers –

PILATE: What!

LUCIUS: That he would come back again. From the dead. Within three days…

PILATE: Oh-hh! This again! Three days, three days! First the elder from Arimathea, now this!

LUCIUS: They - they are apprehensive…

PILATE: Apprehensive?

LUCIUS: What if his followers return to the tomb by night, steal away the body?

PILATE: Ah-hhh…

LUCIUS: They would then be able to spread this fiction among the people: Jesus is risen…

PILATE: Yes…

LUCIUS: Great harm would come of it - a disturbance, perhaps, greater than the one already quelled…

PILATE: And their worry might well become our worry...

LUCIUS: Indeed, Sir…

PAUSE. PILATE PONDERS.

PILATE: Lucius.

LUCIUS: Sir?

PILATE: Go tell them: the Governor of Judaea will not send
            men under his command to guard a grave! He will not
            be privy to this folly…

LUCIUS: Sir…

PILATE MAKES TO TURN AWAY… TURNS
BACK AS A THOUGHT STRIKES HIM.

PILATE: Eh-hh… They have their own guards, have they not?
            Mercenaries? In their pay?

LUCIUS: Why, yes, I -

PILATE: Then let them see to it!

LUCIUS MAKES TO EXIT…

PILATE: Lucius?..

LUCIUS: Sir?

PILATE: What do you make of it all?

LUCIUS: I – I…

PILATE: No, tell me. Seasoned campaigner that you are. What
            is your thinking?

LUCIUS:	I - I do not know -
PILATE:	What!
LUCIUS:	I - I witnessed his death, this Jesus. He died as no felon ever would… ever could.
PILATE:	Hmmm… First my wife… Now my centurion.
LUCIUS:	Sir, I…

PILATE PONDERS A MOMENT. THEN –

PILATE:	Go back down, Lucius. Dismiss them.
LUCIUS:	Sir… And if they -
PILATE:	I have spoken. That is my last word…

LUCIUS BOWS… EXITS… PAUSE.

Three days, eh? Huh… Three days from now I shall be back at base… Caesarea… Sun, sea and a mellow wind, offshore…

HIS WIFE ENTERS AT THE OPPOSITE SIDE, STANDS WATCHING HIM.

'Away from this place of superstitions and dark dissent.

'Shaken the dust of this sinister city from my sandals - oh, so gladly!

Enough! No more pressure from the zealots - of one ilk or another!..

HE TURNS TO EXIT, STOPS WHEN HE SEES THE WOMAN. PAUSE. THEY STAND LOOKING AT EACH OTHER AS THE LIGHTS FADE.

THE END

VEIL

"Veronica makes her way through the crowds and wipes the Face of Jesus with her..."

A drama in two acts
set against the backdrop of the first Good Friday

SEAN WALSH

"Will Sadoc exorcise our son?
Can Caiaphas cure our child?"

PREFACE

Veronica. The young woman who reputedly made her way through the crowds lining the way to Calvary and wiped the face of Jesus with a cloth. Later, she found the facial image of the Nazarene embedded on it.

Traditional? Indeed. Devotional? Doubtless. But without foundation in Scripture.

Was there such a person? Unlikely. Her very name - True Image - Vera from the Latin, Icon from the Greek - suggests a fiction.

But popular devotion - and mankind's basic urge to reach out to the Suffering Saviour, offer Him some gesture of solace, however inadequate, along the Via Crucis - ensured that the legend of Veronica lives on to this day.

So… I placed her in the context of a family unit in Jerusalem at that time, then began to stir the ingredients!

Her mother, Ruth, a good living, hard working jewess;

her father, Azarias, a cleric, legalist, member of the Sanhedrin;

her brother, Misach, possessed, who speaks not a coherent word right the way through the drama until the climax;

her boy friend, Benjamin, an impulsive young man with leanings towards the Zealots;

and Sadoc, another member of the Sanhedrin who seeks to manipulate Azarias at an opportune moment…

Fiction! All fiction! Names culled from the Old Testament!..

In brief: the Passion of Christ as it affected a member of the Sanhedrin and his family...   *- S W*

CAST

AZARIAS:

Late forties, early fifties. A legalist, traditionalist, set in his ways. A strict observer of the Law. A scribe, member of the Sanhedrin. In his own home, quite the disciplinarian.

RUTH:

Younger than her husband, Azarias. A devoted wife, loving mother to Misach and Veronica. In awe, somewhat, of her husband...

VERONICA:

In her twenties. 'Lives at home, subservient to her parents - up to a point. Like her parents, she is torn, stricken, by what has befallen her brother. A lovely, lovable girl reduced to tragedy...

MISACH:

Younger than Veronica - but that is academic. Gaunt, grotesque, slobbering, incoherent - a caricature of the young man he once was. In a word, possessed.

SADOC:

Pompous, corporeal, a member of the Sanhedrin, a status quo yes-man, manipulative, about the same age as Azarias.

BENJAMIN:

In his twenties and in love with Veronica. A hot-head with a big heart. He is anti-establishment, anti-Roman, anti-orthodox Jewry. "An armchair Zealot."

OFFICER:

One of the Sanhedrin militia. Two, three lines.

VOICES "IN THE FRONT ROW":

Several lines. Male, female.

On two, three different occasions as indicated in the script.

THE SET:

The living area in the home of Azarias and his family, somewhere "in Jerusalem."

A table, centre piece... chairs/seats...

A passageway "leads in from outside..." Another passageway "leads into the upper part of the house."

Utensils, beakers, an oil lamp... A side table.

A window in "the fourth wall of the set opens out unto the street below." (Mime, as indicated in the script.)

COSTUMES:

Traditional? Costume drama? Modern?.. 'Depends on the production team – how they see it. A play of Yesteryear or a play for Today?..

In two acts? Yes. But can/may be presented as a one-act piece...

78

ACT ONE

SCENE ONE

SET IN DARKNESS. LIGHT AZARIAS. HE STANDS FRONT
STAGE, RIGHT, AT "AN OPEN WINDOW/PARAPET BATHED
IN MOONLIGHT..."

ENTER RUTH. SHE OBSERVES HIM... APPROACHES...

RUTH: Azarias?.. Azarias?!

AZARIAS: Hmmm?..

RUTH: Up at this hour?.. What - what is it?..

AZARIAS: Oh-hh... Nothing, Ruth. Nothing that is worth the
           telling -

RUTH: Standing at an open window, it gone so cold!..
           Azarias, do come back to -

AZARIAS: Ruth? Ruth, we've lived here all our lives. Have you
           ever seen Jerusalem look more - beautiful?

RUTH: The Holy City of the Chosen People... No. No, never
           so... The stars are diamonds in a velvet sky.

AZARIAS: The full moon of the Passover...

Look you - the Temple! Quiet now. Empty.
Majestic.

Tomorrow it will be thronged with pilgrims,
fellow Hebrews from north and south and the
lands of the farther west -

RUTH: Come to celebrate the Passover in the Mother
City...

You will be there? In the Temple?

AZARIAS: Why do you ask? It is my place...

RUTH: Then you'll need all the sleep you can -

AZARIAS: And there! See! The Praetorium. Constant
reminder of the Roman presence - the
Coloniser...

What do they know of our rites and fasts?..

Behind locked doors they eat and drink and
revel, caring nothing for the one true God, or
the Race he has chosen.

Oh, they sense a spring-tide in the city,

a swelling of Jews in the streets and hostels,

and so they have mounted guards and check-
points, doubled the Sentry on the turrets...

I have it that Pontius Pilate has come from the
coast with full militia to make a show of

of strength - as if the Passover could ever be an occasion of violence...

RUTH: Come, Azarias. I will cover you, keep you warm...

AZARIAS: To what avail? 'Lie open-eyed, awake and restless, marking the minutes and the hours till cock-crow and the dawn chorus? Best leave me as I am...

RUTH: You dreamt again?

AZARIAS: Oh-hhh... A dream so vivid, so tantalizingly real, so horrible..!

RUTH: Oh, my husband! Will it ever end? A sign, portent – what, what is it? What does it mean?

AZARIAS: I wish I knew. Oh, how I wish I knew...
Trapped. Trapped and alone in this pit.

Dark and damp. A pit that reeked of stench and decay... And I could not see!

In the utter and terrible darkness I was blind.

And they knew it! Them - at the top of the pit. They called to me, cried down at me.

Mindless garble... Mocking... menacing...

I was afraid, I who have never known fear,

knew fear then, there in that place.

Afraid to move, stretch out my hand, afraid of what I might touch...

RUTH: No, Azarias! Don't dwell on it! You only
            torment yourself -

AZARIAS: And you, my wife. I also torture you... Oh-hh...

RUTH: See, the dawn is breaking. It will be daylight soon.

AZARIAS: Dawn? Daylight?.. The first blessing in the day of a
            blest man. A man who is blest in his work, his life,
            his family. I am not such a man...

RUTH: Now you speak foolishly, my husband!

MISACH ENTERS... TO ONE SIDE.

Blessed is the man who bears trials and tribulations
with patience.

Blessed is the man who trusts in the Most High Lord.

Such a man, surely, is Azarias the Pharisee.

MISACH MOUTHS WEIRD, INCOHERENT
SOUNDS...

Oh-hh, Misach! My child...

AZARIAS: Your child....Our son....Spawn of the devil.

RUTH: Don't say that –

AZARIAS:	I say it because it is the truth. You know it is the -
RUTH:	Never. Never! Our son is ill, that's all. Very, very ill.
AZARIAS:	So ill, in fact, that the best physicians in Palestine have failed to succour him! The boy is possessed.
RUTH:	You are possessed to say such a thing! You bring your dreams with you into day and see, they taint your thinking! Shame on you, Azarias, that you should say such and such of your own flesh and blood. Our son is in fever, nothing more....
AZARIAS:	A fever that has lasted six months and as many weeks! A fever that makes his flesh cold as the Temple courtyard in winter! A fever that has struck him deaf and dumb, causes him to rant and rave at the very mention of Beelzebub!

MISACH EXCLAIMS IN AGITATION.

	See? The pup knows his patron!
RUTH:	(BREAKING DOWN)
	Oh, Azarias, Azarias! It is not true. What you say of our son cannot be true... cannot be true.
AZARIAS:	"I bring my dreams with me into day and allow them to taint my thinking". Would that were so, woman.

I fly a dream at night only to face a daily nightmare.

The sight of a son possessed. The stench of a full-grown youth so helpless he cannot look to himself. The son of a blessed man? Ha!..

RUTH: He was not always so. My last-born was not always so. He was fathered in a bed of love by a man who had come to know, through trial and error, the art of tenderest love. That is why I love him as I do. Nor could I cease to love him even if I wanted to.

AZARIAS: My son. Misach... He had a hankering, I think, to follow in his father's footsteps –

to learn the law, to expound the law, to teach the people who are bound by the law...

I saw him thus in my mind's eye as he searched the scriptures, learned by heart his very first psalm.

I saw him, in the blind pride that is every father's lawful licence, as a legalist, the greatest doctor in the land. Nay more!

I saw him as a prophet, a man among men, a burning message from on High on his lips, ablaze in his eyes, overawing the Roman scum, leading his people, Israel, out of bondage. In my pride I saw all that.

And then, this... Oh Lord on High, then this!

RUTH: He is still your son.

AZARIAS: This? You tell me this is my son? I tell you, woman –
the day he became like this he ceased to be my son!

RUTH: You can stand there and say that? To think that you
could forget the night he was conceived, the days and
nights, the weeks and months he grew inside me. The
hunger and the passion that seldom left you all that
time, as if you wanted to strengthen him more and
more...

AZARIAS: 'Over. Done with.

RUTH: No, Azarias, no. While our son lives and breathes it
cannot be over. This is flesh of your flesh, blood of
your blood, bone of your –

AZARIAS: This - mine? This is Beelzebub's!

MISACH IN AGITATION AGAIN.

AZARIAS: Beelzebub!.. Beelzebub!!

MISACH IN A FRENZY.

RUTH: Cease, in the name of the Most High, cease!

RUTH HURRIES TO HER SON, SUPPORTS

HIM... BEGINS TO GUIDE HIM AWAY.

There, there, my son, calm yourself... Hush, hush. Be quiet... Come, I will guide you to your pallet... Come with me, my son... Come with your mother, child... You will sleep now. Sleep and rest... Now... Come now... Your mother will put you to bed... Now...

EXEUNT RUTH AND MISACH... PAUSE.

AZARIAS: Oh pity me, Most High Lord.

Have pity on me for thy mercy's sake.

God of Abraham, of Isaac, of Jacob, pity me
and have mercy on me now.

Have I not suffered enough at your hand? Been humiliated enough?

Hear then the prayer of a proud man and give me back my son...

My friends shun my threshold.

My relatives no longer break bread with me.

My voice is no longer heard in the Synagogue.

My fellow Pharisees turn away at my approach...

Today, even today, none but my own family will join me in celebrating the Passover...

Be mindful of thy servant, Lord. Of him and his

family.

Am I not your servant and loyal witness?

One of the chosen few?

All my life I have kept your law.

All my days I have observed even the most minute prescriptions of the Torah.

I have walked in public places, my head on high, conscious of my dignity.

I have been an example to your people, an exemplary Israelite... Always. Always.

I have prayed and fasted, gone in sackcloth and ashes.

All this and more...

And how now do you reward your faithful servant?

You put him on the rack, torture him with dreams, give his son to the devil!

Be mindful at last of your servant, most High Lord.

I entreat you. One blessing I implore.

One blessing, only, I beg of you, Lord above!

Beg... beg!

Give me back my son... Give me back my son!

FADE LIGHTS...

SCENE 2

LIGHT SET. MORNING... (BIRD SONG?) THE LIVING AREA/ROOM...

VERONICA DOWNSTAGE, BUSY WITH A HOUSEHOLD CHORE...

BENJAMIN ENTERS AT THE BACK,

STANDS OBSERVING HER...

VERONICA TURNS OF A SUDDEN:

VERONICA:	(STARTLED) Benjamin!.. Don't do that!
BENJAMIN:	I – Veronica, I -
VERONICA:	Why aren't you at work?
BENJAMIN:	'Passing. 'Took the steps three at a time to, to
VERONICA:	What?
BENJAMIN:	Dw - dwell a moment on, on the most stunning jewess in all Israel!
VERONICA:	Oh-hh! Will you come down to earth, Benjamin?
BENJAMIN:	And who's to say I'm not more rooted in our soil than your father and all his lot? They bow to Rome rule, I embrace the Zealots!
VERONICA:	You're going to be late! -
BENJAMIN:	A patriot am I!

VERONICA:	Some day your bragging will land you in chains. The Romans have eyes and ears everywhere -
BENJAMIN:	Ah-hh! So you do fear for my safety?
VERONICA:	Of course I do, you big - ! Oh, what's the use!
BENJAMIN:	Exactly. I am committed to the Cause.
VERONICA:	And the cause is crazy. And you are mad to have anything to do with it. Mad, Benjamin, mad!
BENJAMIN:	Some day... some day.
VERONICA:	Some day will be like all the other days of revolt: bloodshed and killing without mercy. And afterwards, the wailing of women, the cries of hungry children. I tell you, you are mad to have anything to do with the Zealots...
BENJAMIN:	So?.. I am to turn a deaf ear and a blind eye to the plight of the Hebrews? All is well in Israel?!
VERONICA:	We will see days of freedom and real peace in our land. The Messiah will deliv -
BENJAMIN:	The Messiah? Ha! We have waited his coming for generations. Centuries! I am long past the -
VERONICA:	(SHOCKED... REMONSTRATING...) Benjamin!
BENJAMIN:	Oh, very well. I –
VERONICA:	And who is to say he hasn't already come?
BENJAMIN:	What?

VERONICA:	How do we know that he is not here among us? The Deliverer.
BENJAMIN:	Well, I haven't heard any trumpets lately. The Romans are still in the saddle -
VERONICA:	Did it ever occur to you that fanfare may not be his way?
BENJAMIN:	Did it ever occur to you, my pale-faced darling, that you are spending much, too much, time indoors? Fresh air, Veronica. Fresh and mountain air. I recommend it.
VERONICA:	I have been to, to a Mount.
BENJAMIN:	Mount? Where?
VERONICA:	I'll tell you all about it -
BENJAMIN:	Another time?
VERONICA:	Yes.
BENJAMIN:	Then make that other time tonight.
VERONICA:	We'll see.
BENJAMIN:	I'll come by after work. We'll walk and talk awhile.
VERONICA:	Now will you please go? My father could come at any moment!
BENJAMIN:	I'm on my - I just want to -
VERONICA:	Go! Go! GO!!

EXIT BENJAMIN... VERONICA TURNS
AWAY, SMILING TO HERSELF...
FADE...

SCENE THREE

VERONICA: CHORES...

RUTH: (COMING ON)

Ah-hh!.. Bless you, Veronica. The table set, the places laid, the meal prepared...

VERONICA: 'Twas nothing.

RUTH: 'Tis everything. Without your hand I could not have coped.

VERONICA: Indeed you could, my mother. Well we know it... (PAUSE...)   And you believed him?

RUTH: Hmmm?

VERONICA: Rabbi Sadoc?

RUTH: I had no reason not to. Why should I doubt his word? Besides, he would have nothing to gain by telling a lie.

VERONICA: Nothing to gain! But mother, they have everything to gain! Don't you see? They are out to discredit the Nazarene.

RUTH: Judging by all accounts the man is making fair at discrediting himself.

It is said - and said reliably, mind - that he consorts with publicans, that one of his followers is a tax collector, and that he allowed a woman of the streets to kiss him in public... There, you see? He can hardly be a good man, Veronica.

VERONICA: Was.

RUTH: Hmmm?

VERONICA: Was, mother - was. Levi collects taxes no longer. Now he is called Matthew and follows the Nazarene. That woman has not gone back to her old ways. She - she sins no more.

RUTH: You seem to know quite an amount about this man, Veronica... I suppose you will tell me next you believe in him?

VERONICA: I don't know, my mother. I am my father's daughter. And yet I cannot, will not, close my ears to what I have heard. Of one thing I am certain - he is a good man.

RUTH: So he is a good man. So?.. Your father is a good man. The chief priest is a good man. Rabbi Sadoc is a good man. There are many good and honorable men in Jerusalem - good and honorable because they follow the law.

This man from Galilee, this stranger from the North, does not follow the law: he speaks against it, openly despises all that your father holds dear.

How can a daughter of Azarias the Pharisee stand there and say the Nazarene is a good man? Why your father would be furious, Veronica, if he heard you say such a thing.

VERONICA: Would he? And would he be furious if he knew that I had made my way beyond the gates of the city and through a crowd of men and women to see this man? Then so he may be furious. I have seen Jesus.

RUTH: Veronica! In the name of the Most High! Are you taking leave of your senses or what comes over you? My son goes to the devil, and now my daughter goes to the Nazarene!

Never, Veronica, you would never do such a thing! On your father... let down this house, your family name... The daughter of Azarias the Pharisee mixing with the rabble of the city, staring at the antics of a common magician? Never!

VERONICA: I knew it would be like this! I knew you would not listen to a single word... You are my father's wife.

RUTH: And I am your mother, Veronica. You may have grown to womanhood but I am still your mother. And I forbid you now - 'you mark me, daughter? - I forbid you to approach this man ever again, to see or be seen in his following...

Now go to your room. Remain there until it is time to celebrate the Pasch. Another word about the Nazarene and I shall bring the whole matter to the attention of your father...

VERONICA: The most ordinary, most extraordinary man I have ever seen...

RUTH: Veronica!

VERONICA: His eyes as much as said - "I know you, have

known you from all eternity."

RUTH: Veronica, go to your room this instant!

VERONICA: And his voice. Oh, my mother, his voice! It is the sound of water in deep flood.

RUTH: You... You have never defied me before, Veronica. Is this man's magic so powerful that he can come between us?

VERONICA: As you wish. I will do as you wish, my mother.

SHE MAKES TO EXIT... TURNS BACK:

Mother...

RUTH: I am listening...

VERONICA: You love me very much, do you not?

RUTH: Have I ever given you cause to doubt it?

VERONICA: As you love my father and Misach - your last-born and only son.

RUTH: Amen to that.

VERONICA: Mother?

RUTH: Child?

VERONICA: It... it is commonly said that, at Caphernaum, some weeks ago... Jesus relieved a lunatic boy of the devil.

EXIT VERONICA. FROM THE OPPOSITE SIDE, MISACH ENTERS...

RUTH: Relieved a lunatic boy... of the devil...

               MISACH MOUTHS INCOHERENTLY. RUTH IS
               STARTLED.

RUTH: Oh-hh!.. Heavens, startled by my own son! I must be
               getting old. To think that my own flesh and blood
               could set my heart pounding. I have been calmer,
               betimes, in the presence of a stranger.

               Stranger... Oh, why do I act a part, play a role - as if
               all were well with my world. You are a stranger to
               me, Misach. And I cannot reach you. There is
               something in you, a coldness about you, that is not of
               me or your father. Oh, if I could only reach you, help
               you, bring you back to what you were.

               What a family, what a family! Your sister Veronica
               has done a mad, mad thing. She has run in the wake
               of the prophet from Galilee. You know that? Of
               course, you don't. You don't know at all what
               happens about you... Well it's true, Misach. She has
               been won over by a man who has publicly denounced
               the Pharisees.

               Yes, she has... I can see it in her eyes, hear it in her
               voice. "The most ordinary, extraordinary man I have

ever seen... His eyes, oh his eyes... And his voice is as
the sound of water in deep flood."
Don't you understand, at all? Oh, if I could only talk
to you, Misach. I am deeply worried. Your sister
has been snared by this man, this deceiver, this Jesus -

MISACH BECOMES SUDDENLY AGITATED -
UGLY, SINISTER.

RUTH: Misach, my son, my son! Why do you go on so? I am
            your own mother, why I would not harm you for all
            the world! You are safe with your mother, Misach...
            Safe from all harm. Hush, my son, hush... No need to
            be afraid. All I said was...

            HER VOICE FALLS TO A WHISPER AS IT
            BEGINS TO DAWN ON HER.

            Jesus...

SCENE FOUR

SADOC AND AZARIAS ENTER...

SADOC: Caiaphas is wise, very wise.

AZARIAS: Indeed... Annas, before him, was a wise man.

SADOC: Quite, quite. And Caiaphas says, - act now. Act we
              must or there will be bloodshed in Jerusalem.
              Bloodshed, did I say? A blood bath would be more
              like it. The Romans would descend on us like
              mountain wolves. A great rending of the nation, a
              great scattering of the people.

AZARIAS: And how does our leader propose to avert this - eh,
              national disaster?

SADOC: My, my. You know, Azarias, old friend, the years are
              beginning to catch up on me. I haven't a puff after
              climbing those stairs. I must seat myself... (SEATS
              HIMSELF) Ah, that's better...

AZARIAS: Can I offer you some wine?

SADOC: Wine? Now, that - that would be better still. Not that I
              indulge, you understand. Seldom, seldom indeed. If
              ever. But, after all, it is the great Feast, the day of
              days. Besides, we see each other so very seldom -

AZARIAS POURS WINE, OFFERS A CUP TO
SADOC.

AZARIAS   We seldom see each other, Sadoc, because you never
           darken my door, and because I am not encouraged to
           take my place in the Sanhedrin.

SADOC: No, no! I mean, thank you. Not so, Azarias, not so! I
           have been meaning to visit you these weeks past -

AZARIAS: Months.

SADOC: But pressure of work, you understand. Engagements
           at the Temple. And then this most annoying business
           of the carpenter-fellow from up North. A positive
           nuisance. Mmmm - very good wine if I may say so,
           Azarias, old friend. Very good health to you and to -
           to all your household.

AZARIAS: Does your toast include my son who is possessed by
           the devil?

SADOC: (FORCING A LAUGH) Azarias, my dear fellow,
           you always had a wry sense of humour... Now then,
           where was I? Ah, yes. This infernal nuisance, this
           Jesus fellow, has got to be got rid of. Otherwise there
           will be hell to pay. So says our High Priest. And
           Caiaphas, our Caiaphas, is hardly ever wrong. To
           quote his own very words - *Better that one man
           should die than the entire nation perish.*
           You see, if this uproar continues the Romans will
           look upon it as stirring up the people, open rebellion,
           sedition if you like. And they will act. Nothing more
           certain. And we both know what that means.
           Oh, I shudder at the very thought. No two ways about

	it - the carpenter must die.
AZARIAS:	Die?
SADOC:	Yes, die. You know - puff. Extinguished. For the good of all. We feel it's the only way. Necessary, absolutely necessary, if the race is to survive.
AZARIAS:	And how do you propose to exterminate him?
SADOC:	Oh I say, must you? Rather a painful choice of word, don't you think? We - to put it briefly - we propose to take him, try him, find him guilty and hand him over to the Romans with a strong, indeed a very strong, recommendation that he be - executed.
AZARIAS:	I see... Jerusalem is teeming with people, men and women of the Diaspora, come from far places, east and west, to celebrate the Pasch in the Holy City. It will be like looking for a needle in a hay-stack.
SADOC:	No, not quite. We have a good idea where he will be when we want him... Tonight when the city is sleeping. The High Priest's personal guard will take him. The Sanhedrin will convene - at least as many of them as can be - eh - conveniently -
AZARIAS:	Tonight? But it is highly illegal to hold a trial after sunset!
SADOC:	There are times, Azarias, when I almost despair of you! Caiaphas has said it will be quite in order to try this fellow tonight. And after all, Caiaphas is our High Priest...
	You know, we have much against the Nazarene. His

sorcery, conniving with the devil, upsetting the people, leading them astray, preaching false doctrines and the rest.

Some of all that we could forgive, overlook, condone. But one thing, Azarias, one thing we can neither forgive nor forget: he upbraids us publicly, calls us hypocrites, and challenges our authority.

We are the anointed of the Most High and he condemns us. Now if he were from the Most High he would be one with us, one of us. If he is against us - and nothing in this whole, nauseating mess could be more obvious - then he cannot be from the Most High.

No, Azarias, the man is diabolic, an agent of darkness. So, come the dawn, we will nail this blasphemer to a cross - an apt way of killing a carpenter, don't you think?

May I help myself to some of your fruit? It looks very inviting.

AZARIAS GESTURES: HELP YOURSELF...

AZARIAS: You have words at will, Sadoc, you always had. And

	yet I hesitate. I, I have been out of touch lately. I am hardly acquainted with the finer details of this man's case. I –
SADOC:	But there is no need for minutiae, Azarias. No need, at all. When you consider that Caiaphas is –
AZARIAS:	Yes, yes! Must we have a repetition? Caiaphas is, after all, our High Priest! And Caiaphas says! And Caiaphas is never, ever, wrong!..
SADOC:	Hmmm, excellent fruit. Excellent. I really must make a point of dropping in on an old friend more often. It was surely a sin on my part to neglect you, Azarias, over the weeks. And now that we will be seeing much more of you in future, in the Sanhedrin -
AZARIAS	The Sanhedrin?
SADOC:	Didn't I tell you? Heavens, it clean slipped my mind. Caiaphas has noticed your absence this past while. He wonders at your absenteeism. It would warm his heart, so he says, if again Azarias the Pharisee would take his rightful place in the Sanhedrin.
AZARIAS:	I - I do not know what to say.
SADOC:	Then say nothing, man, say nothing: Come among us once more. Oh, you will be warmly welcomed. That I assure you. You have laboured under a mis-apprehension far too long, far too long. Come back to us, Azarias, and be prepared to shed tears - so overwhelming will be your welcome.

SADOC STANDS, PREPARES TO EXIT.

My thanks for the fruit - and the wine. A repast that will sustain me during the arduous hours ahead... You will come back, Azarias?

AZARIAS: But of course. I -

SADOC: Then what better time than the present. The Sanhedrin will convene as soon as the Nazarene is safely under guard. A messenger will bring you word. Better still, I myself will call in on my way to the house of the High Priest. You will help us get rid of this vermin from Galilee.

AZARIAS: Yes, but –

SADOC: (GOING) History will be made this night. And you will be one of the chosen few who will make it. Aye, Azarias, aye. Tonight all loyal Pharisees will unite in a common front to destroy the common enemy. Think of it, Azarias, think of it - tonight we save our nation. Until then, loyal friend... until then...

EXIT SADOC.

AZARIAS: What to make of it? Why the change of a sudden?.. . Am I to be - manipulated? No, no!.. It would not be honorable...

HE INCLINES HIS HEAD, "LISTENING."

THEN HE MOVES DOWNSTAGE TO ONE SIDE,
MIMES OPENING A WINDOW "IN THE FOURTH
WALL, PUSHING BACK SHUTTERS..."
HE LEANS FORWARD, CALLING OUT:

Ho there! Ho! Why the commotion?..

VOICES IN THE "FRONT ROW..."

- Haven't you heard?

- All Jerusalem has it by now!

- About Lazarus!

- In the village of Bethany!

- He was dead for three days!

- Dead and buried!

- I saw it! With my own eyes!

- Jesus. Jesus of Nazareth raised him from the dead!

- The Messiah has come!

AZARIAS MIMES DRAWING IN THE
SHUTTERS, FASTENING THE WINDOW... HE
CROSSES BACK TO CENTRE STAGE, MUSING
ALOUD:

AZARIAS: A man brought back to life...

A blind man given back his sight...

Now talk of a Messiah...

What - what is afoot in this tormented land?

SUDDENLY, OFF-STAGE, RUTH SCREAMS.

AZARIAS: (CALLING) Ruth! Ruth, what is it? Ruth!

RUTH: (CALLING) Come, Azarias! Azarias?

AZARIAS: (CALLING) Where are you?

RUTH: In the upper room! Oh, come quickly, Azarias! Come quickly!

AZARIAS HURRIES OFF-STAGE... FADE SCENE

SCENE FIVE.

MISACH LIES SLUMPED, MOANING,
WHIMPERING. RUTH KNEELS BESIDE HIM,
TENDING HIS WOUNDS. WATER, BOWL,
SPONGE... AZARIAS STANDS CLOSE BY.

RUTH: 'Cannot understand it. I just cannot understand it. He
            never behaved like this before.

AZARIAS: How did he come by the knife in the first place?

RUTH: I, I may have left it down. I have always been most
            careful. Always dreaded something like this...

AZARIAS: So he came upon a knife and slashed himself.

RUTH: Oh, Misach, why? Why?

AZARIAS: It means only one thing: he grows steadily worse.

RUTH: Not so. This may well be a sign of recovery.

AZARIAS: What! Are you so desperate, woman, that you are
            driven to speak so foolishly? We must watch him,
            day and night: it has come to this... Here, let me help
            you... Where is Veronica?

RUTH: In her room. I sent her to her room for - for speaking
            out of hand.

AZARIAS: You send a full-grown girl to her room for half a day
            because she spoke out of hand? (CALLING, ASIDE)
            Veronica?!.. It must have been quite a speech.

(CALLING) Veronica!

ENTER VERONICA. SHE HURRIES FORWARD -

Your brother, in a tantrum, has cut himself. Help you
mother –

VERONICA: Oh-oh... Oh, dear... Here, let me -

RUTH: If you would just hold this bandage... there...
(PAUSE.)

AZARIAS: You are quiet, Veronica - too quiet. Why do you sulk
so?

VERONICA: Sulk? I do not sulk, my father. If I am quiet it is
because I am sad.

AZARIAS: Oh-hh? And why are you sad?

VERONICA: Be - because of what you and the others plan to do to
a good man.

RUTH: Hush, Veronica. Hold your tongue.

AZARIAS: Meaning what, Veronica - meaning what?

VERONICA: There, that should stop the bleeding. But he is weak,
mother. He needs rest. Sleep and a hot meal.

AZARIAS: Veronica, I asked you a question.

VERONICA: Yes, my father. You asked me a question. And if I
answer truthfully – ? Oh, what's the use of - ? I heard
all: I was in my room, the door ajar, and heard every
word that passed between you and Sadoc.

RUTH: Veronica, how dare - !

AZARIAS: Woman, take your son to his pallet. Let him sleep a while.

RUTH AND VERONICA HELP MISACH TO HIS
FEET. RUTH LINKS HIM OFF, AD-LIBBING.

RUTH: Come, my son, come with your mother... You will
             rest a while now... rest and be at peace...

             EXEUNT RUTH AND MISACH...   PAUSE.

AZARIAS: Hmmm. A daughter of mine, eavesdropping!

VERONICA: It happened quite by chance. I was closing the door of
             my room when a single phrase came to my ears - "the
             carpenter must die." I couldn't move. I didn't want to
             listen and yet I –

AZARIAS: Yet you did. Listen to a conversation that was no
             concern of yours, a professional and confidential
             discussion between two members of the Sanhedrin.

VERONICA: No concern of mine?

AZARIAS: He is not innocent.

VERONICA: Then what is he guilty of? Doing good? Teaching
             love, justice, truth?
             Speaking words that never before came from the
             lips of man?
             Is he guilty of some transgression because he gave
             her dead son back to a widow woman,
             gave sight to a blind man,

gave speech and hearing to a deaf and dumb mute? Is he to be crucified because he relieved a lunatic boy of the devil?!

AZARIAS: That will be enough Veronica!

VERONICA: No, it will not be enough, my father! An hour from now that two-faced faker will call to bring you to the Sanhedrin - because he needs your vote, he and the others who are in on the plot. Don't you see? They are only using you. He doesn't give a fig for you! Why, they all ignored you until now because your son's condition was a slur on their good name. Pharisees? They are parasites!

AZARIAS: Hold your tongue, Veronica. I command you!

VERONICA: Command me? By what authority can you command me to keep silent, watch an innocent man being done to death by men who are jealous of his way with the -

AZARIAS STRIKES VERONICA ACROSS THE FACE... PAUSE.

VERONICA: So now... you have struck me... Did you hope to strike me dumb?

For the first time, the very first time, you have raised your hand against me. And all because I spoke the truth as I know it to be true...

Oh, I honoured you, how I honoured you. I was so proud of Azarias the Pharisee, my father. Because he was an upright man, a scribe among scribes, who walked tall among his people. I was proud of you then. Now - now I am ashamed of you!

SHE TURNS QUICKLY AND HURRIES OFF...

RUTH ENTERS... APPROACHES...

AZARIAS: My household, what comes over my household? My son is given to lunacy and my daughter becomes a vixen overnight. Is there a curse on this home?

RUTH: Will there be a blessing on it this night?

AZARIAS: You, too? No, surely not, my own wife! Surely I can count on your loyalty?

RUTH: Is it true what she says?

AZARIAS: True!? The romantic ramblings of a teenage girl!

RUTH: But you have been asked to attend the Sanhedrin?

AZARIAS: Yes. An emergency meeting has been called by the High Priest.

RUTH: Oh-hh. All very sudden and unexpected.

AZARIAS: Sudden, yes. But not unexpected. This Jesus is a wily fox, it will take the best brains among us to snare him in his speech. My colleagues need me, I will not disappoint them...

RUTH: Veronica is much put out about the Nazarene.

AZARIAS: Three days from now she will have forgotten the entire business. 'Tis her age, that's all. She is a dreamer of dreams...

RUTH: I will go and comfort her.

AZARIAS: Leave her be, leave her be, she will come to herself by and by... It will be dark soon... We will gather to celebrate the Passover. Here, here in this room, as we have done, faithfully, year by year...

And then I will go with Sadoc to the house of the High Priest, take my rightful place among my colleagues. We will sit in judgment on this imposter, trip him up, expose him for what he really is. And then, afterwards... But what happens afterwards will be no concern of mine: it will be for Rome to pass sentence.

Oh, woman, you don't know, you can't possibly know, what this means to me - recognition, renewal, reinstatement. Already I feel ten years younger!

RUTH: But what if it be true?

AZARIAS: What if what be true?

RUTH: What Veronica says, what is on the lips of the common people. What if the Nazarene is, in fact, a good man?

AZARIAS: You speak treachery!

RUTH: I am your wife, Azarias: to you I have sworn life-long loyalty.

Always, over the years, I have been faithful to you.

And I will stand by you now, come what may.

But as sure as I am wife, I am mother also.
And my son, my son lies without - ill, bleeding, possessed.
Aye, possessed! I will not deny it longer. He is the devil's...

And which of your colleagues in the Sanhedrin -
good and honorable men that they may be -
which of them cares a whit for our plight?
And even if they cared, what could they do?

MORIENDO...

Will Sadoc exorcise our son?

Can Caiaphas cure our child?..

DARKEN SET

SCENE SIX.

ENTER VERONICA AND BENJAMIN.

VERONICA: Quickly! Come, quickly!

BENJAMIN: Easy, girl, easy, why the sudden excitement?

VERONICA: My father could come at any moment.

BENJAMIN: Where is he now?

VERONICA: At prayer. My mother keeps vigil at my brother's bedside. Now listen, Benjamin, and mark my words -

BENJAMIN: Now, you listen to me, Veronica. I want to know -

VERONICA: There is no time - We must be urgent!

BENJAMIN: About what, in the name of - ?

VERONICA: Trust me. I will make all clear on the morrow. Now we must act!

BENJAMIN: Look, I –

VERONICA: You know the city well, Benjamin. You know the back streets and the lane-ways.

BENJAMIN: So?..

VERONICA: You, you must lead me to the house of, of Caiaphas, the High Priest.

BENJAMIN: What?!

VERONICA: My mother will retire soon, as is her wont - to be close by Misach should he wake. I'll feign a headache, go to my room, wait a while.

Then - then I'll veil myself, slip out by the side way.

BENJAMIN: Now just a min -

VERONICA: We must do our utmost to save the life of an innocent man!

BENJAMIN: Who?!

VERONICA: Please. Please, Benjamin. Do this for me. This once. Go. Go now!

BENJAMIN: I – Well, I...

VERONICA: Oh, bless you, my love! Now go - go!..

A RELUCTANT BENJAMIN TURNS... EXITS.

VERONICA CROSSES TO A SIDE TABLE, LIFTS A BASKET, BEGINS TO SORT HEAD GEAR: SCARVES... VEILS.

ENTER SADOC... PUFFING... OUT OF BREATH.

SADOC: He was either a scoundrel or a dolt. One way or the other, a rude fellow. I am fortunate to be alive. He came running headlong down the stairway and staggered me against the wall. And without so much as a "beg your pardon" he was gone into the night. A rogue, I'll swear, a rogue and a ruffian.

Oh, my heart, my poor, poor heart!.. I must sit down...

HE EASES DOWN, BREATHING HEAVILY.

Ah-hh... Eh - What could he possibly be up to?

VERONICA: Who?

SADOC: The fellow I'm telling you about, this bouncing ragamuffin!

VERONICA: I have no idea.

SADOC: Well, he was hardly in here, was he?

VERONICA: We... we don't have visitors - as you know...

SADOC: Hmmm. Yes, quite... And now you will be so kind as to tell your father that I am here and in haste.

VERONICA: Yes... 'A minute.

EXIT VERONICA

SADOC: Hmmm... Grapes...They look very inviting... Well... Perhaps one or two...

AS SADOC TURNS TO THE FRUIT BOWL ON THE TABLE MISACH ENTERS, APPROACHES.

Mmmmm... Delicious...

MISACH DRAWS CLOSER, STANDS BEHIND
SADOC... EATING... UNAWARE...
A SOUND FROM MISACH: LOW, UGLY,
SINISTER. SADOC JUMPS UP, STARTLED,
KNOCKING THE FRUIT BOWL TO THE FLOOR.

SADOC: Oh-ohh-oh! Heaven help! Oh Father Abraham!..

MISACH BEGINS TO LAUGH, LOW AT FIRST...
EERIE, OMINOUS... RISING TO CRESCENDO.

SADOC CALLING, FRANTIC.

Azarias! Azarias! Where are you, Azarias?!

RUTH HURRIES IN, GOES AT ONCE TO
MISACH WHO BEGINS TO SUBSIDE.

RUTH: I fell asleep! You must forgive us, Sadoc. I don't
           know what has come over my son of late.

SHE BEGINS TO LEAD MISACH OFF.

He is always so quiet, so terribly quiet... Hush, my
son. Hush... Come with your mother, Misach... come
now... come...

RUTH CONTINUES TO AD-LIB AS SHE LEADS
MISACH OFF.

SADOC... RELIEVED... RECOVERING.

SADOC: Oh, dear... dear me...What a narrow escape. The
            Most High watches over his own, no doubt....

ENTER AZARIAS.

            Ah-hh... Azarias. I fear I've broken your fruit bowl,
            trampled your grapes. It - it slipped from my hands
            when... when -
AZARIAS: The first human sound to pass his lips in months - and
            when I heard it, I knew Hell was rejoicing!
SADOC: Eh - yes. Quite. He - he seems to have a rare fever.
AZARIAS: The simple truth is: he is possessed. And neither you
            nor I nor any scribe in Israel can do a thing about it.
SADOC: Oh, come now, old man. Things are not as bad as all
            that. The power of prayer is great and it is written: the
            prayer of the just man -
AZARIAS: Veronica tells me you have come in haste?
SADOC: Quite. There is no time to be lost. And yet we must
            hasten slowly. The timing is of the first importance...
            May I have some wine?.. Join me?
AZARIAS: Thank you, no. I intend to remain quite clear-headed

tonight... I have prayed long and hard about all this.

JUG, GOBLET/CUP... SADOC POURING...

SADOC: Sorry?

AZARIAS: This plot to kill the carpenter.

SADOC: Plot? Plot, Azarias?

AZARIAS: You know as well as I do that it is a plot. A snare -
            trap to catch and punish an upstart from the north who
            has marred our public image, wounded our pride.

SADOC: Now, really, Rabbi –

AZARIAS: Tell me, Sadoc, tell me the details of your plan to take
            this man.

SADOC: (POURING) Indeed. No doubt it will please you
            Azarias, 'appeal to your legal mind... Sure you won't
            have some wine, old friend?.. No?

            Well, anyway, this fellow came to us, you see... One
            of them, a follower of the Nazarene... A close friend,
            so they say. Comes from a place called Keriot...
            Judas, I think, he called himself.
            Had a foxy look that said as loud as words - "Give
            me money." So we did. Thirty of the best. It was
            nothing. Nothing for what we got out of him. Right
            this very moment he is leading the guards to where
            Jesus has bedded down for the night... a place called
            Gethsemani...

Within the hour he will be standing in the Hall of Judgment, bound hand and foot. We will have him - and we will not let him go...

But isn't it laughable, Azarias, to think of it. Doesn't it really tickle you - one of them coming to us... One of his very own selling him out for thirty pieces of silver. Just goes to show what a lousy lot they are. Scum.

ENTER AN OFFICER OF THE SANHEDRIN

OFFICER: Rabbi....

SADOC: Ah, officer. What news?

OFFICER: The watch reports: a torch waving aloft on the slopes of Olivet.

SADOC: Ha! The signal. Our trap is sprung. The Nazarene is our prisoner. (TO THE OFFICER) Await us in the street. You and your guards will give us safe conduct to the house of the High Priest.

OFFICER: Rabbi.

THE OFFICER SALUTES, EXITS.

SADOC: See! It is working - beautifully. Truly, the Most High guides us, protects us from our enemies. Let us go and deal with this Jesus.

You know, I can hardly wait to see what he looks like. 'Wonder if he has horns and cloven hooves. Ha, ha, ha!..

LAUGHTER DIES.

Come, come, Azarias! Don't look so forlorn. Your heart will lift at the sight of your old comrades. This is your hour, Azarias...

AZARIAS: (ASIDE) My hour or the hour of darkness...

SADOC: You will take your lawful place in the Sanhedrin once more -

AZARIAS: (ASIDE) I will take my lawful place...

SADOC: You will be listened to by the leaders of the people, and you will speak out in defence of the law and the prophets as never before.

AZARIAS: (ASIDE) 'Speak out as never before....

SADOC: Then come. Let us hurry. Caiaphas awaits us...

AZARIAS: I struck her - this evening - for the very first time I raised my hand to her –

SADOC: Who?

AZARIAS: Veronica. My daughter, Veronica. And all because she said Jesus is a good man.

SADOC: (LAUGHING) But that's the whole point, don't you see? Jesus is not a good man! If he were a good man then we could be even now in our beds with our wives... But he is not a good man... And so we must be up and active, sober and celibate... defending all that we hold dearest.

Jesus a good man! Ha, ha, ha!..

Jesus, that's a laugh!..

FADE LIGHTS.

SCENE SEVEN

RUTH AND VERONICA ON THEIR KNEES AT
THE TABLE, WIPING THE FLOOR, PICKING UP
FRUIT, PIECES OF THE BROKEN BOWL.
ON THE TABLE A LIGHTED CANDLE/LAMP.

RUTH: Really, Veronica, you should have known better. The
             way you spoke to him. I could scarce believe my ears.

VERONICA: It was without malice, I assure you. I love him dearly
             - as I love you, my mother. Yet - oh, I am confused! I
             had no idea what I was going to say until I had said it
             - as if something within me came to life and emanded
             a hearing.

RUTH: What's said is said. In the morning you will make your apologies. He is a good man; he will forgive - and forget.

VERONICA: Apologise for saying what I know to be true?! Apologise because I voiced my deepest convictions? Say I'm sorry I stood up for an innocent man in his absence? My father would be further insulted by such an apology. He is not a hypocrite - nor am I...

RUTH: You are hard, Veronica - I had no idea how hard. Your father and I have always been good to you. We do not deserve such coldness...

But I will not argue with you more... I am weary, oh, so weary. It has been a long day. May the Most High bless us all this night... May he guide and strengthen your father...

VERONICA: My father - gone to the Sanhedrin?..

RUTH: But a while ago. They say it may go on into the early hours... I don't know, I do not know. You are confused, I am confused... Your father is confused - at least so I suspect... The Nazarene has thrown our household into confusion...

Gave sight to a man born blind, did he? Drove the devil out of a lunatic boy? May be. May be... Can everyone be wrong? If he can work miracles then let him work his greatest miracle tonight. Else he will surely die.

Sadoc is out for his blood. Sadoc is mean... mean.

May the Most High be with my husband this night. I would not wish him to have anything to do with meanness....

VERONICA: Mother, I -

RUTH: Go to bed, child. Your mother has said far too much - she has voiced her inner thoughts in a rare way... Go to bed and sleep... In the morning I shall have forgotten my words... as you will... if you are wise... It is in the hands of the Most High now... Be it so...

EXIT RUTH... VERONICA WATCHES HER GO.

VERONICA: Goodnight, my mother... You mean me well... you and my father... But tonight I cannot sleep... tonight I must do what I can for the Nazarene... for you and my father... and Misach.

SHE CROSSES TO THE SIDE TABLE, SELECTS A VEIL FROM THE BASKET...

ENTER BENJAMIN. SHE TURNS, SEES HIM.

VERONICA: Oh-hh! I -
BENJAMIN: Change of plan.
VERONICA: What?

BENJAMIN: Sorry, my love, I'm not moving until I know what we are about -

VERONICA: But we can't delay! There's no time to -

BENJAMIN: To tell me? Then we'll make time.

VERONICA: Oh, Benjamin... I've told you: you are to lead me to the House of the High Priest.

BENJAMIN: And if I do, what then? (PAUSE) Veronica?

VERONICA: When... when we get there, I - I don't know what we'll do...

BENJAMIN: Hmmm... As I thought...

VERONICA: I'll think of something! This minute he is in their their hands, the trial may have already begun, and you stand there -

BENJAMIN: Who is in their hands? Who are they? What trial?

VERONICA: Jesus. Jesus of Nazareth. He has been taken by the Temple Guard. The Sanhedrin plan to kill him.

BENJAMIN: Oh... Oh-hh.

VERONICA: Now will you move?

BENJAMIN: (MUSING) The prophet - or so he styles himself...

VERONICA: We've got to act.

BENJAMIN: Much talk of miracles.

VERONICA: He's a good man, Benjamin, a good man.

BENJAMIN: Good for him, good for you. Some of our people have been keeping an eye on him, and we don't like what they report.

VERONICA: They will kill him, Benjamin.

BENJAMIN: So they will, so they will. When those shrinks put

their shaggy beards together, they can make
rain fall in Hell.

VERONICA: Well, then - ?

BENJAMIN: Look, Veronica: if your Jesus is such a great man
why hasn't he struck a blow for Israel?
If he is a true leader of the people why hasn't he done
something about the Roman occupation?
If he is such a great worker of miracles why hasn't he
blasted the invaders to Hell before now?

VERONICA: I won't -

BENJAMIN: No, let me finish, just let me finish....
Do you know what he's said? Publicly, mind. "Love
your enemies. Do good to those who hate you. Bless
those who curse you. And pray for those who treat
you with contempt".

VERONICA: Well, if he -

BENJAMIN: He wants me to love the Romans, bless the tax
collectors, pray for the Rabbis - the sycophants of the
Synagogues, druids who never did a day's work in
their lives, parasites who live off the people! Love,
bless, pray - for them? The man's mad!

VERONICA: They're going to crucify him, Benjamin. A few hours
from now.

BENJAMIN: He'll have company.

VERONICA: What?

BENJAMIN: Barabbas has been sentenced... Now there's a real
man. Barabbas, our leader. A man who organised a

thousand spears up in the hill country - and led them
against a Roman phalanx... So he failed - but failed
honorably... Your prophet from the fishing village
wouldn't know one end of a spear from the other!..
Barabbas is to go up with the sun - and we can't do a
thing about it.

VERONICA: I know nothing of Barabbas. But of Jesus I do know.
He –

BENJAMIN: Forget him. As he will be forgotten a few days from
now. He is a dead man.

VERONICA: I must go to him. If you won't come with me,
then I – I...

BENJAMIN: Go half-way across the city at dead of night on a
fool's errand?! There will be guards at every
entrance, you won't get within a stone's throw. Why?
Why so foolhardy?

VERONICA: I don't know, Benjamin. It's here, in my heart - an
urge I cannot contain...

BENJAMIN: And tomorrow that urge will still be there: somehow,
somewhere on the way to Calvary, you'll press
forward through the crowds and, and... Oh, I know,
you, Veronica. Know the nature in you. And it makes
me love you all the more.

VERONICA: You'll do this for me, Benjamin - if you really love
me.

BENJAMIN: Now you put me on the rack.

VERONICA: Please, Benjamin. Please!

BENJAMIN: We - we best walk quickly. Stay close...

SHE IS VEILING HERSELF AS THEY EXEUNT.

ENTER MISACH...
HE SLOWLY CROSSES TO THE TABLE,
PICKS UP A BUNCH OF GRAPES, CRUSHES
THEM BETWEEN HIS HANDS, DROPS THEM
TO THE FLOOR, OPENS HIS HANDS:
THEY ARE RED...

EERIE, SINISTER LAUGHTER... LOW.

THEN HE LEANS FORWARD, BLOWS OUT THE
CANDLE/OIL LAMP.

HIS LAUGHTER RISES TO CRESCENDO AS
THE LIGHTS FADE.

FADE LIGHTS...

ACT TWO

MORNING. (BIRD SONG...)

AZARIAS CENTRE STAGE, IN DEEP
THOUGHT...

RUTH ENTERS... WATCHES HIM...

AZARIAS: (THINKING ALOUD) No more... No more.

RUTH: (APPROACHING) Azarias?..

AZARIAS: Ah, Ruth... I will not talk of dreams again. It is done,
            Ruth, over and done with. The nightmare is no more.

RUTH: Oh, I thank the Most High for that! You were sorely
            tried...

AZARIAS: The sounds and the pit and the endless dark... No
            more. But oh, what a price I have paid for it!

RUTH: What? I fail to follow..?

AZARIAS: Last night I took my place, my lawful place, in the
            Sanhedrin - and knew that I was in the pit, the pit of
            my dream. I listened to my colleagues - whispering,
            murmuring, denouncing, ranting and raving - and
            asked myself, Where before had I heard these
            voices?..

RUTH: Oh, my husband.

AZARIAS:	I could not move. 'Could not raise my voice in his defence - much less my hand. And Sadoc sensed it. Sadoc, that cunning lecher, sensed it. He called for silence, then turned to me: "Azarias knows the law, what says Azarias?"
RUTH:	Oh, Azarias...
AZARIAS:	All eyes were upon me - save the eyes of the one who stood on trial. And I said - I said, "It is a point of law. The issue at stake is clear. He has spoken blasphemously. He is guilty of death." And like a chorus from hell they rose to their feet and shouted - "Death! Death! Death to the blasphemer!"
RUTH:	No, my husband. Do not go on so. You scourge yourself - and me...
AZARIAS:	I was afraid, afraid of losing my position... My prestige was at stake - my prestige as a scribe and doctor of the law. His life was at stake!..
RUTH:	If - if it is true that he blasphemed -
AZARIAS:	We all blasphemed last night! All of us who demand-ed blood in the dead hours of darkness. We reduced the law of the Most High to sheerest mockery.
RUTH:	But why did you not -
AZARIAS:	Why did I not speak out? Defend him? Defend the law and all that I hold dearest? Why did I not have the courage of my convictions? Why did I not cry out - 'But this is wrong. The entire procedure of this court contravenes the law

A vote cannot be taken in the absence of Nicodemus.

The witnesses are guilty of most obvious perjury!'

RUTH: Cease, Azarias. You are racking me -

AZARIAS: I'll tell you why:

because all my life I have done as they did,

spoken as they spoke,

thought as they thought.

All my life I followed the party line -

and rated it as virtue...

All my life - until last night.

This man challenged me as I have never before been challenged.

He stood there, eyes downcast. Stood in silence.

Oh, that silence - it will sear me to my dying day.

Not a word from him, not so much as a word, as the accusations were recorded against him.

And yet, even thus, he was a challenge to me.

And I failed - failed him, myself, the law, the prophets...

I crawled on my belly and said -

"Yes, yes! Here, here! I second the motion!

Let him die and be damned!"

Don't you see, woman? I am not a man...

not a man...

AZARIAS BREAKS DOWN, SOBS... RUTH COMFORTS HIM

RUTH: Oh, my husband... my husband...

AZARIAS: Not a man... not a man... I could have been... failed, failed... coward that I am... less than a man...

RUTH: Don't say that, don't say that! You are my man - and I know you better than you know yourself. Nothing you can say or do will convince me that you are less than what you are in my eyes, my heart. You are the man I married many years ago. I was proud of you then, as I am proud of you now.

AZARIAS: Ruth... You are good for me.

RUTH: I have always tried to be good for you - and for our family.

AZARIAS: My family... He stood there, bleeding. His wrists were cut where the guards had bound him... And I thought of Misach. I did what I could for Misach, but for Jesus of Nazareth I did nothing.

RUTH: It would have been of no avail. Nothing you could have said or done would have changed their minds. They were bent on blood.

AZARIAS: If only you knew how true your words are... Oh-hhh. She was right.

RUTH: Who?

AZARIAS: Veronica. Our Veronica. She has more courage than her father, has the courage of her convictions.

RUTH:	She is only a girl. She cannot realise how much there is at stake for you - for all of us....
AZARIAS:	She acted without thought for herself - or fear of any consequences. She is another Ruth.
RUTH:	She really believes in him, Azarias, she really believes in the Nazarene.
AZARIAS:	And because she said so, I struck her...
	It was during the interrogation: he answered, fearlessly.
	And a servant of the High Priest, a lewd fellow, turned on him, struck him across the face...
	I can still hear the sound of that blow, see his head jerk under the force of it...
	Then he looked up – "If there was harm in what I said tell us what was harmful in it; if not, why do you strike me?.."
	I sat there stunned, rent in a thousand pieces... and thought of Veronica.
RUTH:	No more of that. Come... I will make breakfast.
	SHE GUIDES HIM TO THE TABLE. HE SEATS HIMSELF... PAUSE.
AZARIAS:	How sleeps Misach?
RUTH:	Well.

AZARIAS:	And Veronica?
RUTH:	She is - up and about.
AZARIAS:	So early?
RUTH:	She - she said she could not sleep.
AZARIAS:	Then summon her. We will break the fast together.
RUTH:	I - I think she is out of doors...
AZARIAS:	You may be sure of it. The Nazarene in peril and Veronica to sleep soundly in her bed? Unthinkable! Woman, woman, would you deceive an aged and broken man? I know the girl well. She is her mother's daughter.
RUTH:	Benjamin is a good -
AZARIAS:	Benjamin is a young fool. A quick tongue in a hot head! He escorts her?
RUTH:	Yes.
AZARIAS:	Then let him guard her well. Else he will answer to me. Where did they go?.. Well?
RUTH:	To the house - they went to the house of the -
AZARIAS:	High Priest?
RUTH:	Yes.
AZARIAS:	I should not be surprised at that - and yet I am. I wonder... where are they now, how goes it with him?.. And you, Ruth? How did the night pass with you? Did you sleep well?
RUTH:	None too well.
AZARIAS:	I do not doubt it. How could you close your eyes

	knowing your daughter was afoot, your husband on trial for his very manhood -
RUTH:	Knowing that an innocent man was being done to death by -
AZARIAS:	Bigots, Ruth. Bigots. Among whom I am numbered with honour. They will decorate me for my defence of the law...
RUTH:	I will bring you a hot drink.
AZARIAS:	No matter. The hottest drink could not drive the chill from my bones. It is a numbness of the spirit, it were best be dead...

ENTER VERONICA... BENJAMIN "HANGING BACK..."

AZARIAS:	Ah, Veronica!.. You are just in time. Your mother is about to serve a meal... Well, are you going to stand there all morning?.. Come in, come in! And bring your young man. Let us break bread together.
RUTH:	Come in, child. Benjamin, you are welcome. Sit down, both of you. You must be tired.
VERONICA:	I – I'll help you, mother.
RUTH:	(GOING) Nonsense, Veronica. It is already prepared. Bring Benjamin to the table, bring him in.

VERONICA AND BENJAMIN JOIN AZARIAS.

AZARIAS: Well, Benjamin. I haven't seen your face for many a
             day... And how many Romans did you kill last night?
BENJAMIN: Last night my sword was pointed at the Israelites. I
             could have drawn blood from my fellow men.
AZARIAS: You were there?
BENJAMIN: In the courtyard. They would not allow us further.
AZARIAS: Of course. The - trial was enacted behind closed
             doors.
VERONICA: We saw him when he was brought out - he passed
             quite close to where we were. .It was terrible -
AZARIAS: You will see him no more.
VERONICA: My father - ?
BENJAMIN: He means they will crucify him. Today. At noon.

         RUTH, OFF STAGE, SHRIEKS HYSTERICALLY

AZARIAS: (RISING)   What? what the -
RUTH: (SCREAMING) Azarias! Azarias!?
AZARIAS: What - what is it?!

         ENTER A TERRIFIED RUTH. SHE HURRIES TO
         HER HUSBAND.

RUTH: Misach! Where is Misach?
VERONICA: What?
RUTH: There is someone - something - in there. But it is not
             my son!

134

AZARIAS: Benjamin, shut that door. Bolt it. Now.

BENJAMIN: Aye, Rabbi!

BENJAMIN JUMPS TO IT. MIMES BOLTING,
LOCKING A DOOR.

VERONICA: It grows dark - and cold.

AZARIAS: What? But, but the sun still shines! How can - ?

BENJAMIN: Oh-hh... Such a stench!..

SADOC, OFF STAGE, IS HEARD CALLING:

SADOC: Azarias!.. Azarias!

ENTER SADOC

Ah, there you are!.. The most wonderful news, old
man! The Romans have given in. They fell for our
little ruse, walked right into our trap!
Oh, Caiaphas is wise, wise. He briefed our men well.
They moved among the crowd, gave a common voice
to the mob. "You are not a friend of Caesar's," they
shouted, "if you release this man!"

Pilate paled. Oh, you should have seen him pale! He
simply couldn't wash his hands of the whole affair,
quick enough. The Nazarene is ours.

Even at this moment he is being scourged. He'll look a bloody raw sight when we've stuck him up. He'll be a raw - ha, ha, ha! - a raw Nazarene, eh, Azarias? Ha, ha, ha!

HIS LAUGHTER TRAILS AWAY...

I say, have I said something? You haven't had bad news, I hope?.. My word, it is dark in here...

OFF STAGE: A SUDDEN RENDING OF WOOD... CRASHING...

A GROTESQUE BENJAMIN ENTERS.

CRIES, SCREAMS, AD-LIBBING...

BENJAMIN: Don't look, Veronica, don't look!
VERONICA: How can I not?
SADOC: Heavens! The lunatic boy - worse then ever! The eyes! Father Abraham, the eyes!
MISACH: As good as dead, is he? Good, very good.
RUTH: He speaks!
AZARIAS: But not with the voice of our son.
MISACH: We speak with many voices: we are many...

SADOC:	You know, I really ought to be going.
MISACH:	You will go. One day. And you will be very welcome. We will make you at home. You have done your work well, pharisee. You have followed our instructions carefully...
SADOC:	I have no idea -
MISACH:	Of course, you haven't. None of you have! Fools! Puppets! Actors in a play within a play! When I direct nothing goes wrong. It has been a supreme success.
BENJAMIN:	If I hadn't heard it with my own ears -
MISACH:	Seen it with your own eyes! That's the wonderful thing about you mortals: you're rotten with pride. The same pride that makes us crawl on our bellies and eat dust.
AZARIAS:	Genesis.
MISACH:	Correct. First Book. Moses, by the way, did not write Genesis. He merely laid the foundations. The script came much later. You rabbis are way out there.
SADOC:	Is he telling us our business?
MISACH:	Be quiet, you pompous fool. You have done what we deemed necessary. Now you are expendable. You can die now - or later. We are content to wait.
SADOC:	Azarias, are you going to stand there and -
MISACH:	Yes! He is! Because he is rooted to the spot. As you are, yes-man. Even if you wanted to move, you blubber of fat, you could not!
	It will be done now... soon... very soon.

Then let it be done. Let him die. Lucifer, our

Master, we serve you well...

VERONICA: Let me go, Benjamin. Let me draw near him -

BENJAMIN: No!

MISACH: Don't touch us. You hear? Don't touch us! Take one

more step in our direction, and we will rend you

asunder!

Where did you get it? It's his, isn't it? It belongs to

him, doesn't it? Then it touched him! Take it away,

throw it away, destroy it! You hear us? It must be

destroyed! Already it burns us! Must be destroyed!

You hear? Must be destroyed!

You are her father, you spawned her! Then command

her, command her, we say: tell her to destroy it!

No, you won't open your mouth, will you? But then

you didn't open your mouth last night either, did you?

You could have spoken but you didn't - you failed,

failed, failed! And your failure will live with you all

your days and all your nights, will scourge you, sear

your conscience, destroy your peace!

It was we who gave you dreams by night - and the

sight of a lunatic boy by day. Well, the dream is no

more. Instead, a memory, the memory of the night

you denied - Him.

MISACH ROUNDS ON RUTH:

Look at her! See! The virtuous woman, the faithful wife, the devoted mother, the good housekeeper! Shall we tell them the truth, woman, tell them that after your second child you ceased to be a woman - put your husband out on grass while he was still in his manhood?

Shocked, are you? Shocked? Or shamed? And not a word out of you, in your own defence, you self-elected spinster! Oh, this is virtue, indeed! You will have your reward - wife!..

HE TARGETS BENJAMIN

And so to Benjamin! Stout-hearted, patriotic Benjamin! You spoke your lines beautifully, we grant you that. But you know - and we know - you are so much better at shifting women than shifting the Romans out of Israel!
BENJAMIN:
Why, you - !
MISACH:
We know you, know you well. So why keep up the act? Be yourself, for once. Grow up! Why, your whole life 'til now has been an act! 'A patriot am I!' And yet at the first whiff of commitment, at the least sign of danger, you are gone into thin air!
The young man with a way with the girls, the young man

with the big problem and the small spine - that's our
Benjamin.

And you're not a bit choosey, betimes, are you? Oh,
he knows the byways and the side streets, does our
young buck! Why, just the other night he laid the
widow woman who does his wash, gave her good
cause to return to her laundry, eh, Benjamin?

BENJAMIN: Lies! Filthy rotten lies! –

HE TAKES AIM AT VERONICA:

Why, you look hurt, my dear. Pained. Rather tragic.
Upset because you weren't the first... But you have
only yourself to blame: we could have spared you all
this - simply left you with memories and fake
illusions.

But you insisted on going there last night. And you
insisted on bringing that, that, back with you!

VERONICA: Let me touch him with -

MISACH: Touch us and you die. I swear it!

AZARIAS: By whom?

MISACH: By Satan - who else?

VERONICA: You are the devil.

MISACH: We are - the cold... But you are - hot. So very, very
hot. Why, even as a child you watched your brother –

whom we now happily inhabit...

EXCLAMATIONS OF ANGER FROM AZARIAS
AND BENJAMIN.

Don't touch us! I warn you, don't touch us - or you
will burn in Hell before we do!

It's all your doing, this, you slut! We had no intention
of breaking the cold war. We were quite content to be
as we were. But you insisted on speaking about him!
You insisted on going there last night! And you
insisted on bringing back that - !

You, you, you! It's all your fault. Curse you! And
curse Him! Aye, aye, Beelzebub! We curse Him. We
curse Jesus of Nazareth! We curse Him and His
mother and all his followers!
And we curse you, you scheming vixen. We curse
you from the depths of Hell!

AZARIAS: You would curse my daughter -?
MISACH: Be quiet!
AZARIAS: Hardly. You may be a devil out of Hell, and last night
            I may have gone in fear of you, followed your
            directions. But now it is day, and this is my house:
            you will not curse my daughter! Benjamin!
BENJAMIN: Aye, Sir!

AZARIAS: I need you –

BENJAMIN: Oh, Rabbi!

AZARIAS: Hold him, Benjamin.

AZARIAS AND BENJAMIN CONVERGE ON
MISACH, GRIP HIS ARMS, GRAPPLE HIM.

MISACH: Don't touch us! I have all the strength of Hell in these
                    sinews –

VERONICA: Down, keep him down! Let me touch him with this - !

MISACH: Look at the whore! See where she comes!
                    We are pure, pure! We want nothing to do with her!
                    Keep her away from us. She is filthy, filthy!
                    She carries disease. Believe us, we speak the truth.
                    She is the greatest carrier in this rotten city!

BENJAMIN: Hurry, Veronica! We can't -

VERONICA: There! Now!

SHE HURRIES FORWARD, OPENING A
CLOTH...

MISACH: Ah - a - a – ah! No, no, not that! His blood is on it!
                    Blood. His blood! No, no, never! It cannot, must not
                    be true! Must not be true!
                    Back there? Not there? Not back there? Not yet, not
                    yet! We entreat you, Lord Jesus, we entreat you!.. His
                    blood, it is his Blood!..

142

Ah-hhh-hhhhhhh...!

ONE LAST CRY OF SHEER DESPAIR AND
MISACH GROWS LIMP... THE MEN AND
VERONICA MAKE ROOM FOR RUTH...

RUTH: My son, Misach... my son, my son.

RUTH CRADLES BENJAMIN IN HER ARMS.

BENJAMIN: Lord Jesus. He called out - "Lord Jesus."
VERONICA: Oh, it was horrible... what he said was horrible.
AZARIAS: The devil is the father of lies. So it is written. Let us
            all remember that this day.
RUTH: This day and always... Misach, Misach...
VERONICA: It was his blood.
BENJAMIN: 'Lord Jesus." As if he were a king.
RUTH: He lives. Azarias, our son lives. He breathes as before
            - and his eyes are the eyes of my child.
AZARIAS: The devils have left him.
VERONICA: Because I touched him with a cloth.

MISACH MAKES A NATURAL SOUND, SIGHS...

RUTH: Oh, my son, you are well, you are well.

SADOC: I really don't know what to say –

AZARIAS: Then say nothing but go.

SADOC: Go? I don't quite -

AZARIAS: Go, go. Get out! Out of my house and don't come
                back! Ever.

SADOC: Well, really - !

RUTH: My husband has asked you to leave, Sadoc. In no
                uncertain terms. This also is my sentiment. You have
                outstayed your welcome. Now, please go.

SADOC: I see. Well, I'll go. Good riddance, that's what I say.
                You were a damned nuisance, the lot of you. An ill
                reflection on all decent, upright Pharisees.
                Why, I've never been so insulted! All right, I'll go.
                But mark my words: I don't quite know what's been
                going on among you lot but the Sanhedrin is going to
                hear from me. Caiaphas shall have a full report.

BENJAMIN: Oh, to Hell with you and Caiaphas!

SADOC: Why, I never – !

                EXIT SADOC

RUTH: Oh, Misach, Misach...

AZARIAS: Veronica, bring water.

VERONICA: At once.

                VERONICA CROSSES TO THE SIDE TABLE,
                POURS WATER FROM A JUG INTO A CUP,

144

CROSSES BACK TO RUTH, HANDS IT TO HER.

RUTH: My son has come back from the dead.

AZARIAS: The living dead...

RUTH: Now, Misach... Drink... Easy... There now...

VERONICA: They handed him over to the guards, there in the
             courtyard. By the open fire. They blindfolded him,
             struck him on the face, again and again, demanding
             that he prophesy... Bent the knee, mocked him.
             Oh, how my heart went out to him!
             And when they brought him away, I picked up the
             cloth they had used to blindfold him....this cloth.

BENJAMIN WALKS DOWNSTAGE AND MIMES
OPENING A WINDOW, LEANING OUT.

BENJAMIN: (CALLING) What news? Ho, you down there?!

THE VOICES "IN THE FRONT ROW" RESPOND:

    - The Romans are bringing Jesus to Calvary.

    - They have left the Preatorium –

    - He is to be executed -

    - The crowds are thick by the East Gate.

- Crucified - with two others.

- But not Barabbas. He has been released.

- By the will of the people.

- Jesus goes up in his place.

BENJAMIN MIMES CLOSING THE WINDOW,
CROSSES BACK UPSTAGE.

BENJAMIN: Barabbas... free... Our leader goes free!.. I should be
            overjoyed... I - I am more confused than ever...

VERONICA TURNS, CROSSES TOWARDS THE
EXIT, TURNS BACK WHEN RUTH CALLS:

RUTH: Veronica!
VERONICA: I must go to him. Can't you see that? I just cannot
            stand here and –
RUTH: But the mob - !

AZARIAS: Let the girl go. Her heart is already with him.

VERONICA: My father.

RUTH: Veronica! You are forgetting yourself: your veil.

VERONICA TURNS BACK, PICKS UP HER VEIL
AND IS SCARFING HERSELF AS SHE EXITS.

RUTH: Aren't you going with her, Benjamin?

BENJAMIN: She will be safe enough. There are mercenaries
                    everywhere. She doesn't need me now.

HE CROSSES OVER, TURNS BACK ON:

The miracle-worker has worked another miracle - he
has come between us.

EXIT BENJAMIN.

AZARIAS BENDS, PICKS UP THE CLOTH THAT
VERONICA USED IN THE EXORCISM
SEQUENCE, IT IS STAINED RED...

AZARIAS: Such is his power... Then who is this... Have we all of

            us made a terrible...? Oh, I do not know...

RUTH: That he has done great good for all in this household,

            that we do know, Azarias.

            MISACH MAKES A WARM, NATURAL

            SOUND...

            AZARIAS, STILL HOLDING THE CLOTH,

            MOVES TO HIS WIFE'S SIDE, PLACES A HAND

            ON HER SHOULDER.

MISACH: Mo-mother?.. My - my mother?..

RUTH: Yes, my son, yes...

            I am your mother...

            You are home now, Misach -

            back to us...

THE END

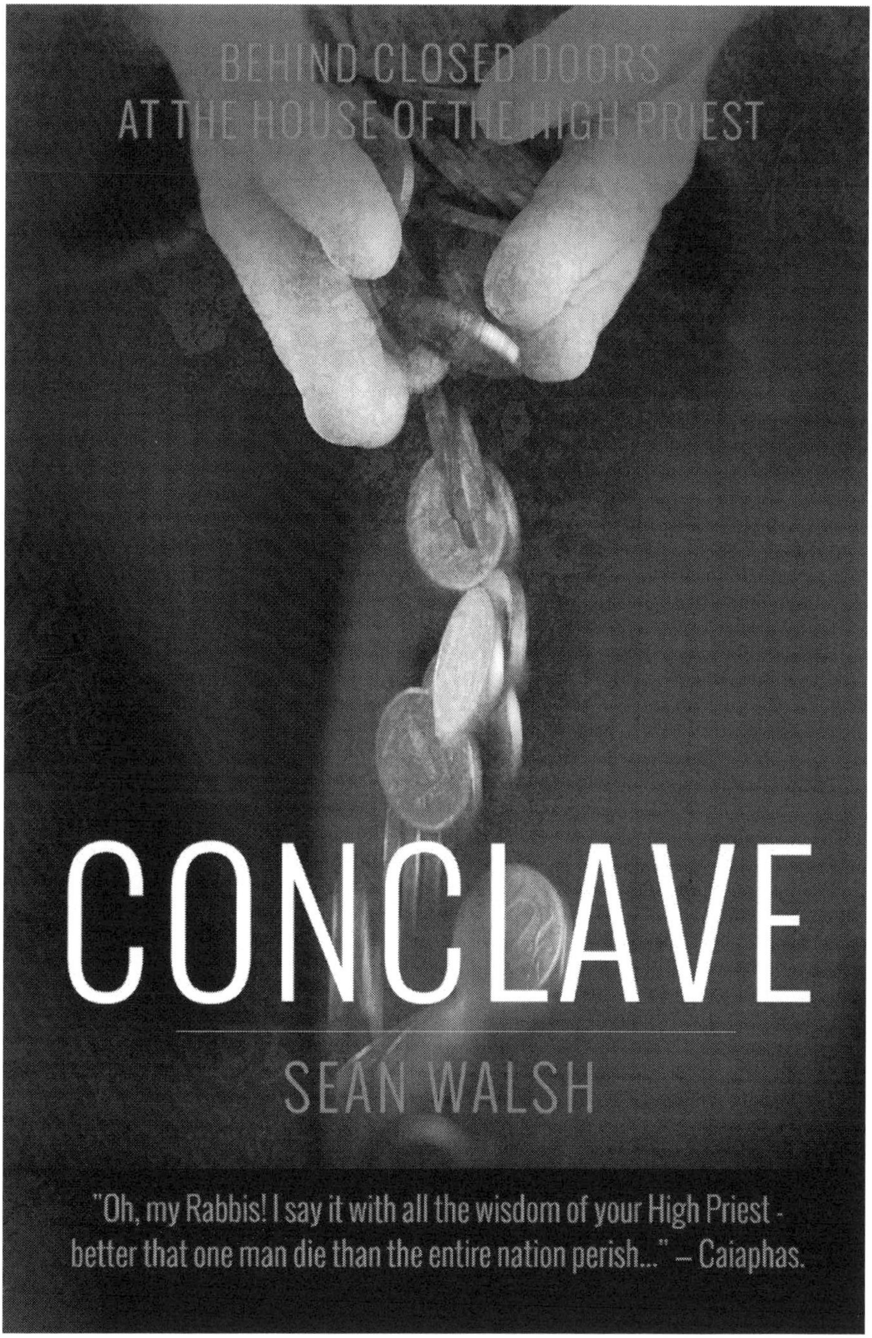

"Dare anyone tell me that this Jesus is the Messiah!"

AUTHOR'S INTRO

Men meet behind closed doors to report, discuss, plan a strategy to protect themselves from an external threat, secure their power-base, ensure their hold on office - even if that means resorting to bribery, putting a certain spin on given facts/events...

As such, it transcends a particular time and place, could be set just about anywhere in the world wherever power-brokers meet in cabinet, conclave...

And though it is based on the gospels - with particular emphasis on the Passion narrative of Matthew - it can be seen as a drama about men anywhere, at any time, willing to go to any lengths to protect their status quo...

Executive suits, shirts, ties? Or costume drama?.. Optional.
(If the latter, Caiaphas would wear a distinguishing insignia of office; the other four dress uniformly.)

The Officer of the Temple Guard wears a police/military uniform - but not one that would identify him with a particular country, place, time...

In contrast, Judas is poorly dressed - tinker, traveler, mendicant? - adding to the repugnance of the Executive...

THE SET

The board room/conference room in the House of the High Priest. From time to time a smaller area to one side comes into play – anteroom, study, scrolling area?..

Conclave may be mounted on a conventional stage or In The Round... I have stayed with a "modern version" throughout; if a director opts for a costume production then stage directions etc., will need to be changed, accordingly...

CAST

CAIAPHAS: High Priest and Chief Rabbi.

JORAM:
SADOC: Members of the Sanhedrin, close to
AMON: the High Priest.
AZOR:

TWO SERVANTS One Male, One Female.
(As the script indicates...)

JUDAS ISCARIOT

ZACH: Soldiers of the
ACHIM: Temple Guard.

AN OFFICER OF THE TEMPLE GUARD.

ACT ONE: Takes place during Thursday, Good Friday.

ACT TWO: Takes place over a longer span – months,
perhaps years?

PREFACE

Conclave centres on a group of religious leaders, the Jewish Sanhedrin, who are so determined to preserve the status quo, from which they benefit so greatly, that they will do all in their power to eliminate anyone who threatens it. They are so secure in their possession of the truth that they are prepared to crush anyone who claims to embody a fuller version of that truth.

I am reminded of an exchange between Jesus and the Pharisees in John's gospel: *'Surely we are not blind, are we?'* Jesus said to them, *'If you were blind, you would not have sin. But now that you say, "We see", your sin remains'* (John 9:41). Caiaphas, whose determination to eliminate Jesus drives those around him, claims to be acting in the interest of the people when, in reality, he is protecting himself and his circle.

Another verse from John's gospel comes to mind: 'One of them, Caiaphas, who was high priest that year said to them (the Sanhedrin), *"You know nothing at all! You do not understand that it is better for you to have one man die for the people than to have the whole nation destroyed."* (John 11:49-50).

In that same gospel, one of the religious leaders, Nicodemus, distances himself from his peers, saying to them, *'Our law does not judge people without first giving them a hearing to find out what they are doing, does it?'* (John 7:51). There is such a Nicodemus-like figure in this play, a member of the Sanhedrin. Such people who challenge the cosy consensus have only one prospect, banishment.

This play, while rooted in the gospels, brings a very contemporary feel to the age old conflict between those in authority who want to protect their position and those prophetic voices who proclaim a word of truth that demands to be heard.

- Fr Martin Hogan,

Lecturer in Sacred Scripture,

Mater Dei,

Dublin City University.

ACT ONE

SCENE ONE

STAGE DARK.

LIGHT CAIAPHAS AS HE ENTERS TO ONE SIDE... BEGINS
TO MOVE AROUND AND THROUGH THE AUDITORIUM...

CAIAPHAS

Jesus, huh?.. Jesus!.. How dare he!.. What gall! What insufferable
gall!.. 'Has the sheer audacity to come here - here - to our Holy
City!.. To Jerusalem!.. 'Enter our gates in triumph - his way strewn
with palms by a despicable ignorati - asses following an ass - hailing
him as the very Messiah!.. Jesus!

Messiah, huh?.. A Messiah from Galilee!?.. Galilee of all places!
How bloody absurd! How preposterous!.. When the true Messiah
comes he will be one of us, one with us. But of course! Absolutely!

But this, this upstart - this pretender from the country - is not of us,
not one with us! Indeed, he shuns our company, treats us with open
disdain, obvious disrespect...

And even now he is in our Temple - our Temple! - preaching his perfidious heresy... the gawking gullible hanging on his every word... Oh, Father Abraham! The thought of it! Near the very Holy of Holies, this blow-in from the North is holding forth, teaching right and wrong, declaring that he is the Way, the Truth and the Life!..

Well, enough is enough. At this very moment, chosen members of my Sanhedrin are mingling with the crowds, noting his every word, recording the least detail... And at the first opportune moment, they will set traps for him, put him to the test, trip him up, snare him in his speech, expose him for the sham that he is...

CAIAPHAS STEPS UP UNTO THE STAGE, TURNS TO THE AUDIENCE.

And when they have seen him off, they will return here to report to me, Caiaphas, Chief Rabbi and High Priest of Israel...

EXIT CAIAPHAS... DARKEN ACTING AREA...

SCENE TWO

ENTER JORAM, AMON, AZOR, SADOC. THEY LINE UP
ABREAST, FRONT STAGE, SET DOWN THEIR BRIEF CASES,
SPEAK DIRECTLY TO THE AUDIENCE...

SADOC

Master, we know that you are direct in your talk, in your teaching -

JORAM

That you hold no one in awe, making no distinction between man
and man -

AMON

But teach the way of God in all sincerity -

AZOR

Tell us, then: is it right that we should pay tribute to Caesar? -

SADOC

Or should we refuse to do so?

PAUSE. THEY LOOK AT EACH OTHER, CONFER...
THEN SADOC SEARCHS, PRODUCES A COIN, THROWS IT
INTO THE AUDITORIUM.

JORAM

Why, why Caesar's...

AZOR

Yes. Yes, indeed. The image on the coin is that of Caesar...

SADOC

None other than the Emperor... (PAUSE) Oh-hh...

THEY LOOK AT EACH OTHER, DISCONCERTED. THEN:

AMON

Tell us: what is the authority by which you do these things? -

SADOC

Yes. Yes, and who gave you this authority?.. (PAUSE)

AZOR

John, John's baptism - ?

JORAM

Did it come from Heaven - ?

SADOC

Or, or from men?..

PAUSE. THEY LOOK AT EACH OTHER, CONFER. THEN:

AMON

We, we do not know...

PAUSE. THEY LOOK AROUND, LOOK AT EACH OTHER,

WHISPER...

THEN THEY PICK UP THEIR BRIEF CASES, EXEUNT IN

DISARRAY.

SCENE THREE

LIGHT THE ANTE-ROOM TO REVEAL A PC/TABLET ON A
COMPUTER DESK. CAIPHAS SEATED, SCROLLING.

CAIAPHAS (READING ALOUD, SLOWLY...)

If a prophet or a dreamer of dreams
arises among you
and offers to do a sign or wonder for you -
and the sign or wonder comes about -
and if he then says to you -

Come, then, let us follow other gods -
whom you do not know - and serve them -
you are not to listen to that prophet
or to the dreams of that dreamer...

That prophet or that dreamer of dreams
must be put to death,
for he has preached apostasy
from Yahweh your God...
You must banish this evil from among you...

CAIAPHAS STOPS, STANDS, PONDERS.

The fifth Book of the Pentateuch... Deuteronomy, thirteen...

HE TURNS, MAKES TO EXIT...

'Banish this evil... 'Put to death... must be put to...

DARKEN THIS AREA.

SCENE FOUR

LIGHT MAIN AREA. ENTER IN HASTE JORAM, AMON, AZOR, SADOC. THEY GROUP, WELL LEFT OF CENTRE, MIME URGENT CONVERSATION...

ENTER CAIAPHAS, FAR RIGHT...

ONE OF THE GROUP TURNS, SEES CAIAPHAS, TURNS BACK, MOTIONS TO THE OTHERS... THEY BREAK UP, TURN, MOVE SLOWLY TOWARDS CENTRE-STAGE...

CAIAPHAS
Well?.. So?..

HE CROSSES, SEATS HIMSELF AT THE TOP OF THE TABLE, GESTURES TO THEM TO BE SEATED. THEY DO SO.

CAIAPHAS
Huh. I have only to look at your faces...
JORAM
We, we carried out your instructions to the letter, High Priest.
SADOC
'Did as you bade us. 'Bided our time and then, when I saw my chance, I put it to him, directly -

AZOR

The question we had agreed: what was his authority - and from whence did it come?..

CAIAPHAS

So?

JORAM

He - he did not answer us, directly.

SADOC

Never. We could never have him give a direct answer. Ever -

AMON

Instead, he put to us a question -

CAIAPHAS

Yes?

SADOC

About John the Precursor -

AZOR

Did his baptism come from Heaven - or from men?

CAIAPHAS

Ah!.. And how did you respond?

JORAM

 We, we did not know quite what to -

AMON

Had we answered, from Heaven, he could then have asked us -

AZOR

Why did you not believe in him? -

SADOC

And had we said from men, the people might well have turned on us

CAIAPHAS

But of course. They look on the Baptist as a prophet... So?

JORAM

We, we said we did not know. And he rejoined -

AMON

Neither will you learn from me by what authority I do these things.

CAIAPHAS

How very cunning!.. And the people?

AZOR

'Applauded him, mocked us...

CAIAPHAS

And the Roman snare? Is it lawful to pay tribute to Caesar or not?

JORAM

Again, he would not say yea or nay – 'asked instead to see a coin of the Realm.

CAIPHAS

Indeed?

SADOC

So I cast a coin at his feet -

AZOR

Then he queried the inscription on it -

AMON

And when we responded, Caesar's -

JORAM

He said, why then, render to Caesar the things that are Caesar's -

SADOC

- and to God the things that are God's...

CAIAPHAS

'Trumped!

SADOC

And again the people applauded him, derided us...

CAIAPHAS

Hmmm... This does not augur well for further confrontation.

SADOC

Indeed. I, for one, would be reluctant to challenge him ever again.

CAIAPHAS

A rout. A veritable rout... My fellow Rabbis, publicly humiliated. I grow more angry by the minute.

SADOC

And further still...

CAIAPHAS

Hmmm?

AMON

He castigated us, Caiaphas.

CAIAPHAS

What?!

JORAM

Openly. For all to hear -

AMON

Oh, what he said! What he said!

CAIPHAS

Tell me... Tell me!

AZOR

'Cursed, denounced us! -

SADOC

'Called us liars, hypocrites! -

AMON

Whited sepulchres! -

CAIAPHAS

How dare he! How! - And the people?..

SADOC

'Stood in awe of him -

AMON

Open-mouthed. Taking in his every word -

JORAM

Never before had we been spoken to in such a manner.

AZOR

But more...

CAIAPHAS

More? What more?!

AZOR

Even as we made to leave -

SADOC

Slipping away, confused, confounded -

AZOR

He called after us - "Jerusalem, Jerusalem!" -

JORAM

"Still murdering the prophets, and stoning the messengers

that are sent to you!"

AMON

And his final words - "Behold, your house is left to you, a house uninhabited..."

CAIAPHAS

A house... uninhabited?..

SADOC

What could he have meant?

AMON

The Temple?

AZOR

Hardly. Our Temple has never been so popular with the common people.

AMON

Then here, perhaps?

SADOC

The House of the High Priest?

JORAM

Who knows? The fellow speaks in riddles.

CAIAPHAS

This we do know. This Jesus, this self-styled prophet, is a danger to us all - undermining our authority, drawing the people away from us.

                      MURMURING... ASSENT...

SADOC

The Temple coffers will empty! Our very livelihood in jeopardy! -

CAIAPHAS

Oh, devilish clever, I grant you - picking and choosing from the Scriptures, ignoring this, emphasizing that - but a shyster for all that!.. Does anything good come out of Galilee?

AZOR

No! Never!

AMON

Then he is a fraud!

SADOC

If we leave him go unchecked he may well cause an uproar -

AMON

Instigate an uprising -

JORAM

Incur the wrath of Rome -

SADOC

Bring upon us the very venom of Caesar -

AZOR

Destroy all we have built up, built upon -

CAIAPHAS

I say it, my Rabbis! I say it with all the wisdom invested in me as your High Priest: better that one man die than the whole nation perish!..

RHURBARB... ASSENT.

SADOC

Well said, oh High Priest!

AZOR

But how? How do we..?

JORAM

Arrest him, put him on trial -

AMON

Find him guilty -

SADOC

Condemn him to...

AZOR

Die?..

JORAM

Rome alone can pass sentence of death.

CAIAPHAS

Then we will deliver him to Rome. Once we have laid hands on him, we will charge him before the Procurator.

SADOC

Witnesses aplenty to bolster our demand that he be crucified.

CAIAPHAS

Torn limb from limb... blooded... destroyed.

SADOC

Annihilated.

AZOR

Nothing left of him, nothing at all...

CAIAPHAS

And that will be the end of it.

SADOC

And the sooner the better!

JORAM

I counsel caution, my brothers. Let us hasten slowly. Jerusalem is thronged with visitors - from east and west - and the farthest corners of the Diaspora -

AZOR

Of course, yes! 'Come to celebrate the Pasch in the Holy City -

AMON

If we lay hands on the Galilean at the Passover -

JORAM

There might well be a tumult among the people -

SADOC

They could turn against us -

CAIAPHAS

Ah-hh, the collective wisdom of the Sanhedrin! I never cease to marvel!.. Yes, let us bide our time.

ENTER SERVANT.

When the Feast has come and gone - when the tribes have dispersed - then, my hierarchs, then we will move against the enemy!..
(CALLING) Yes, what is it? Can't you see we are..?

SERVANT

There is a man without, Rabbi, who would speak with you, urgently.

CAIAPHAS

Man? What man?

SERVANT

He, he says he is - one of them -

SADOC

What!?

SERVANT

A follower of, of -

JORAM

Jesus?

SERVANT

Yes...

AZOR

One of them - here?! -

JORAM

At the House of the High Priest?!

SADOC :

How dare he! -

AMON

Send him away, show him the door! -

CAIAPHAS

No wait!.. (PAUSE) 'Could be... this could be something, indeed...

Why would one of them come here - here above all places - unless..?

SADOC

Unless?.. Caiaphas?

CAIAPHAS

'Only one way to... (CALLING) Show the fellow in.

EXIT SERVANT...   MURMURING... RHUBARB...

CAIAPHAS

Come now, come... Let us be united in this... It may be that...

ENTER JUDAS. HE STANDS, HESITANT...

Step forward...

'Far enough... 'You have a name?..

JUDAS

Judas. I, I hail from Keriot.

CAIAPHAS

So..? Be brief.

JUDAS

I, I am one of those nearest to him. To Jesus. One of the Twelve...

CAIAPHAS

Yes?..

JUDAS

I was in the Temple when he... I saw your faces, the anger in your eyes.

CAIAPHAS

And?..

JUDAS

And but a while ago he allowed a woman to anoint him.

AZOR

Oh-hh?

JUDAS

'Head and body. With precious ointment...

JORAM

Hmmm -

JUDAS

Ointment that would have fetched a goodly sum on the open market. Alms given to the poor -

SADOC

Of course...

JUDAS

He, he is going mad! He will drag us all down! To, to perdition!

CAIAPHAS

Come - to the point!   (PAUSE)

JUDAS

If, if I lead you to him, how - how much will you pay me?..

RHUBARB. AGITATION. MURMURING...

JORAM

Ha! I thought so!

SADOC

Not such a wise Jesus after all!

AZOR

A traitor in his company and he does not know it!

AMON

And he calls himself a prophet?!..

CAIAPHAS

So... Let us confer...

THEY WHISPER AMONG THEMSELVES, URGENTLY. THEN:

We will guarantee you... thirty pieces of silver...

JUDAS

Thirty!? As little as -

CAIAPHAS

Our first and last offer.

JUDAS

But, but -

SADOC

Not a penny more -

JORAM

Take it or leave it... (PAUSE)

JUDAS

I... I accept...

MURMURS OF APPROVAL.

CAIAPHAS

Good. Very good... Now...

We will place the Temple Guard on standby. When you come again

it will be to lead them to Jesus of Nazareth. Agreed?

JUDAS

Yes.

CAIAPHAS

Then go. Leave us.

JUDAS

The money - when will I..?

CAIAPHAS

When he is our prisoner - and not before...

JUDAS TURNS, MAKES TO LEAVE... TURNS BACK AT:

Oh, and Judas?..   (PAUSE)

When you come again it will be for the last time. We won't want to see - or hear from you - ever again...

EXIT JUDAS...   MURMURS OF APPROVAL...

Oh-hh... Pardon me if I vomit... What a contemptuous wretch!..

JORAM

Thirty pieces of silver - the price of betrayal? I can scarce believe my -

AMON

In exchange for the one he calls his Master!

SADOC

And what Master - what manner of man - would allow such scum into his company, be one of his circle?

AZOR

Jesus, huh! Jesus...

AMON

'Calls himself a prophet? A Messiah?!..

SADOC

Why, the fool cannot see through one who walks at his side, breaks bread with him!..

CAIAPHAS

Oh, my Rabbis, if any of you had any misgivings about this Jesus of
   Nazareth, let him banish them now, once and for all, after what we
   have witnessed here this night...

MURMURS OF ASSENT.

Now. It is time. Let us adjourn to the Inner Room.

CAIAPHAS STANDS UP.
THE OTHERS FOLLOW SUIT.

All is in readiness, prepared by my servants... The lamb roasted, the bitter herbs and unleavened bread laid out, the wine at hand... Then come, my Rabbis. Let us together celebrate the Passover...

THEY BEGIN TO MOVE OFF STAGE...

SADOC

Amen to that -

AZOR

As we have done and will continue to do -

AMON

After the way of our forefathers -

JORAM

Until the advent of the true Messiah...

DARKEN SET AS THEY EXEUNT...

MALE VOICES, OFF, SINGING *THE HALLEL*...
THEN THIS SINGING DIES AWAY...

SCENE FIVE

LIGHT THE CONFERENCE ROOM, AS BEFORE...
THE GANG OF FIVE ENTER FROM THE BACK...

JORAM

It worries me...

SADOC

What?

JORAM

We, we had already determined not to move against the Galilean at
the Passover -

AZOR

Ha! But a while ago, Joram, who was to know this fellow from
Keriot would approach us, play into our hands? -

SADOC

An offer we could hardly refuse? -

CAIAPHAS

Expediency, my dear Joram - expediency! Would you rather I had
turned him away, forfeited the chance to rid ourselves of the
Nazarene for ever more?..

SADOC

No, of course not! If we seize him tonight, put him on trial, find him
guilty of outrageous blasphemy -

AMON

We could be at the gates of the Roman fortress, come the dawn!

AZOR

Demanding the death penalty!..

JORAM

So... so many pilgrims in Jerusalem! 'Could go against us?

CAIAPHAS

People can be managed, a multitude manipulated. Besides, how are we to know for certain if this betrayal will run its course?..

AZOR

Hardly tonight. The full moon of the Passover is high in the sky -

AMON

Time we made for our beds...

SADOC

Where all well-minded Israelites already are.

MURMURING... ASSENT.

CAIAPHAS

Joram?.. Still troubled?

JORAM

Oh-hh... One minute we are going in one direction, the next in the opposite. It, it's as if we were being pulled one way, then another - almost, as it were, against our collective will...

CAIAPHAS

Joram, Joram! You ponder far too deeply!.. Are we not endowed with the wisdom our office confers on us? Are we not the chosen ones of the supreme Sanhedrin - skilled alike in the study of the scrolls and the reading of men's hearts?..

SADOC

Indeed and indeed, High Priest!

CAIAPHAS

Are we not masters of our own destiny?..

MURMURS OF APPROVAL...

ENTER SERVANT.

CAIAPHAS

Yes, what is it?

SERVANT

Rabbi, the, the...

CAIAPHAS

Come, speak up!

SERVANT

The man who, who sought audience with you, urgently -

CAIAPHAS

What about him?

SERVANT

He, he's without in the forecourt -

CAIAPHAS

Dolt! Show him in! Hurry!

SERVANT   (GOING) Sire!..

AZOR

Tonight? Is it to be this very -

SADOC

As good a time as any -

AMON

What better time? The city is sleeping -

SADOC

The pilgrims long since abed -

JORAM

Unless..?

CAIAPHAS

Unless what?

JORAM

He's come to bargain for more money?

SADOC

Nonsense! The price was struck!..

ENTER JUDAS.

CAIAPHAS

Come forward...

JUDAS APPROACHES... STOPS.

So... Judas Iscariot... We are waiting...

JUDAS

The, the one you seek is on the slopes of Olivet -

CAIPHAS

You are certain?

JUDAS

Even as I speak he is at prayer in the Garden of Gethsemani, a plot of land that -

CAIAPHAS

Azor! -

AZOR

High Priest?

CAIAPHAS

Go quickly! Call the Officer of the Guard. Have him muster his men, armed and bearing torches. Do it - now!

AZOR   (EXITING)

At once, Caiaphas! -

AMON

Mount Olivet? At this hour? Why would he..?

SADOC

In hiding - what else?

JORAM

It will be pitch up there. How will the guards know for certain who to arrest?

SADOC

Yes. Yes, how will you point him out?

JUDAS

Eh-hh... I, I will greet him with a kiss.

CAIAPHAS

What?

JUDAS

Him - and him only. The man I kiss will be the one you -

CAIAPHAS

I see... Very well. Now leave us. Wait in the forecourt.

JUDAS

The money? When do I get my -

CAIAPHAS

When he stands before us, bound and under guard.

JUDAS

But I -

CAIAPHAS

You will lead my militia to your Master. But be warned: if you fail to deliver him into their hands, it will go ill for you. Now go.

EXIT JUDAS.

AMON

I will remember that face to my dying -

CAIAPHAS

Sadoc?

SADOC

High Priest?

CAIAPHAS

When the time comes - when the Nazarene is our prisoner - pay him off... But do it aside. I have no wish to set eyes on that, that...

SADOC

As you wish...

CAIAPHAS

'Betrays his Master with a kiss? For a bag of coins? Oh, Father Abraham! My flesh crawls at such abomination...

ENTER AZOR

AZOR

The guards are at the ready, High Priest, the Officer awaits your command.

CAIAPHAS

Good. Then let him lead out. To Olivet, urgently. The informer to go with them. Once in the Garden of Gethsemani, he will greet the Galilean with a kiss. Arrest and return, directly.

AZOR   (LEAVING)

At once...

JORAM

Should not some of us go with them? To make certain -

CAIAPHAS

No. No, we will wait here... We all know how wily is this Imposter. If we are to trip him up, snare him, we must summon all our cunning, stay alert through the long hours that lie ahead...

Now. Amon, have the servants light a fire in the courtyard. Then go with Sadoc and Azor - and you, Joram. Call what witnesses you can. And summon the other Rabbis. Bid them come here with all speed.

And no excuses! Here without fail! This night I demand a full assembly of the Sanhedrin!...

EXEUNT JORAM AND SADOC, AMON AND AZOR.

And once we have him we will not let him go - this side of the grave...

SCENE SIX

LIGHT SET. CAIPHAS AND CO IN THE CONFERENCE ROOM.
SOME SITTING... SOME STANDING AROUND...

AMON

They should be there by now.

SADOC

And back. What's keeping them?

JORAM

Unless he slipped the net, made good his escape?

AZOR

As he did before when we made to seize him.

SADOC

'Faded away among the crowds, hid himself.

CAIAPHAS

'No crowds on the Mount of Olives. 'But a few of his followers to support him.

AMON

Iscariot may have melted in his resolve? -

AZOR

At the last minute?..

CAIAPHAS

With my militia watching his every move? I doubt it...

ENTER SERVANT.

SERVANT

They come, Lord High Priest! The Temple Guard approaches!

CAIAPHAS

Have they a captive or not?

SERVANT

Indeed! 'Bound and in chains!

CAIAPHAS

Then see to their needs. Prepare a supper for them in the courtyard.
And have them bring the prisoner to the ante-room hard by the Hall
of Judgment -

SERVANT   (GOING)

Amen, High Priest...

AD-LIBBING... VICTORY!

AMON

He is ours, Caiaphas!

AZOR

He will not denounce us now! -

AMON

Mock us now! -

SADOC

Call us hypocrites, whited sepulchres! -

AZOR

Humiliate us -

AMON

Now he will be in fear of us -

SADOC

Oh, well he may tremble!..

JORAM

Eh-hh. If I may make a suggestion, High Priest...

CAIAPHAS

Yes, Joram. What is it?

JORAM

Should we not wait until morning, hear him out in the light of day?

CAIAPHAS

Oh, Joram, Joram! Are you, too, from Galilee?.. So... The witnesses await, the accusers are at hand?

SADOC

Indeed -

CAIAPHAS

Then to it. Let the trial commence!..

RHURBARB... ASSENT, APPROVAL.

EXEUNT AZOR, AMON, SADOC, JORAM.

CALLING AFTER THEM:

I will join you anon...

CAIAPHAS STANDS IN A CIRCLE OF LIGHT AS THE SET DARKENS.

So now... Now, Galilean...

Mock my elders?

Humiliate my scribes?

Ridicule my colleagues?

Embarrass my doctors of the Law?..

When you so do, you do as much to me...

And at your peril, Jesus of Nazareth...

At your peril...

DARKEN SET.

SCENE SEVEN

LIGHT AN AREA TO ONE SIDE.

SADOC AT A SMALL TABLE, COUNTING OUT COINS.

JUDAS STANDS A LTTLE WAY OFF, OBSERVING.

SADOC

... twenty seven, twenty eight, twenty nine... Correct?

JUDAS

Yes.

SADOC

Take it.

JUDAS STEPS FORWARD, SCOOPS UP THE COINS.

Now go...

JUDAS

Eh-hh...

SADOC

Yes?

JUDAS

Must I go through the Courtyard?

SADOC

What?

JUDAS

Is, is there another way out?

SADOC

Why do you ask?

JUDAS

I have no wish to see - or be seen - further.

SADOC

Huh... There is a side entrance. 'Left along the corridor as you go
out, then left again. You'll see the door...

JUDAS MUMBLES A 'THANK YOU'...

Your final exit, Iscariot. We never saw you, heard of you. We do not
even know you exist. You understand?.. You were never here.

EXIT JUDAS.   DARKEN SET.

SCENE EIGHT

LIGHT A SPACE TO THE LEFT OF THE MAIN AREA.
ENTER CAIAPHAS AND AZOR, EARNESTLY CONVERSING...

CAIAPHAS

It does not go to my liking, Azor.

AZOR

Oh?.. Eh, there are other witnesses in waiting -

CAIAPHAS

False, Azor, all false - and you know it.

AZOR

What he said about destroying the Temple! There are two who will testify -

CAIAPHAS

They are not agreed. Such accusers would not survive a Roman scrutiny... No, something more is needed, else he could well slip our noose.

AZOR

Hmmm... If only we could rouse him to speak, commit himself?

CAIAPHAS

Small hope of that. Still...

AZOR

A frontal attack - direct challenge - might catch him out..?

CAIAPHAS

Perhaps... I hate him, Azor, hate him as never before I hated any man. And not, mark you, because of his so-called miracles. Or because he has drawn the people away from us. Or because he treats us with disdain, confounds us with tricks of the tongue, humiliates us in public...

AZOR

Then... then why?

CAIAPHAS

Because, Azor, because he claims to be the Son of the Most High.

AZOR

Oh, be assured we are, all of us in the Circle, at one with you in that.

CAIAPHAS

It sticks in my craw, revolts me. And that is why I will not rest until he has been rent on a cross, bone from bone, blooded, destroyed beyond recognition...

AZOR

Amen to that, High Priest.

CAIAPHAS

So... if all comes to all, I will confront him... Come. Let us go back.

AZOR

And if he denies all claim to the Messiahship?

CAIAPHAS

Why, then, we must conjure up a different strategy.

AZOR

And if he assents - says he is, in truth, the son of the Eternal One?

CAIAPHAS

Then he is a dead man...

EXEUNT CAIAPHAS AND AZOR. DARKEN SPACE.

SCENE NINE

LIGHT THE CONFERENCE ROOM.
ENTER JORAM, AMON, SADOC AND AZOR - JUBILANT.

SADOC

I could scarce believe my ears! -

AMON

From his own lips - out of his own mouth!

JORAM

We have heard with our own ears! -

AZOR

'Seen with our own eyes! -

SADOC

'Stands self-convicted! -

AZOR

And all because our High Priest, in his great wisdom -

JORAM

And with all the power of office invested in him from on High -

AMON

Put it to the prisoner, adjured him by the living - !

SADOC

To tell us - directly and under oath - whether he be the Christ - !

AZOR

And when the fool responded, said what we dearly needed to hear -

AMON

Our leader was beside himself with rage! -

JORAM

Down all the years I have never seen him so furious! -

SADOC

'Tore at his very clothing! -

CAIPHAS ENTERS, HOLDING HIS JACKET AND TIE.

AZOR

Oh, well done, High Priest! -

AMON

A good night's work, Caiaphas! -

JORAM

A direct hit, Chief Rabbi! -

SADOC

Oh, wise is Caiaphas, so very wise...

CAIAPHAS (BREATHLESS WITH ANGER)

He - has - spoken - blasphemously!..

MURMURING ASSENT.

Mark well his words:
"You will see the son of man seated at the right hand of the Power
and coming on the clouds of Heaven."

JORAM

Precisely, Caiaphas. Those were his exact -

CAIPHAS

What, then, is your finding?..

AZOR

Why, the issue at stake is clear -

AMON

There is no denying the Law -

JORAM

For such a blasphemy as this -

SADOC

The penalty is death!..

CAIPHAS

We are agreed?

ALL

Agreed!

VICTORIOUS ASSENT, APPROVAL...

DARKEN SET.

SCENE TEN

THE SMALLER AREA/ROOM...

JORAM, DIVESTED OF JACKET AND TIE, SITS AT A P C,

WATCHING THE SCREEN, TAPPING KEYS...

ENTER AMON. HE STOPS UP SHORT WHEN HE SEES

JORAM.

AMON

What on earth!?... Joram?..

JORAM   (STARTLED)

What!?.. Oh, Amon!.. I did not hear you -

AMON

Scrolling?. At this hour? In the name of - !

JORAM

No. No, it's nothing - just a thought...

AMON

What?

JORAM

What he said, the Nazarene, when our High Priest adjured him to tell

us -

AMON

Yes, yes! What about it?

JORAM

"You will see the son of man seated at the right hand of - "

AMON

No need to quote me chapter and verse - I was there, remember? I know what the Deceiver said!

JORAM :

Well... it occured to me, Amon, that somewhere in the Scriptures there are words uncannily similar.

AMON

Oh, Joram, Joram! Always out of step! Forever at a tangent!

JORAM

But, I -

AMON

Does it matter? And should you, perchance, come upon a similar sentence, what will it matter?

JORAM

Yes. Yes, I suppose you are -

AMON

Look you! The others are assembling in the Conference Room, Caiaphas will be wondering where we are. Then come! Enough of conjecture! This is a night for deliberating - not scrolling!..

JORAM

Yes. Yes, of course. I -

AMON   (GOING)

Make haste, Joram. Let us away...

JORAM

At once!..

JORAM STANDS, MAKES TO FOLLOW AMON.

HE CHECKS THE COMPUTER A FINAL TIME, LOOKS AT THE SCREEN - STOPS...

Oh... Oh-hh...

HE SEATS HIMSELF, STARING AT THE SCREEN... HE SPEAKS SLOWLY... HESITATING EVER SO OFTEN... BREAKING THE SENTENCES...

"And I saw, coming on the clouds of heaven, one like a son of man.
He came to the one of great age and was led into his presence.

On him was conferred sovereignty, glory and kingship...
And men of all peoples, nations and languages became his servants.

His sovereignty is an eternal sovereignty which shall never pass away.
Nor will his empire ever be destroyed..."

HE GETS SLOWLY TO HIS FEET.

Daniel... The Prophet, Daniel... Seven... Thirteen...

"And I saw, coming on the clouds of heaven, one like a son of man.

HE PONDERS A MOMENT, THEN TURNS AND SLOWLY EXITS...

SCENE ELEVEN

LIGHT THE CONFERENCE ROOM. CAIPHAS AND THE
OTHERS, DIVESTED OF THEIR JACKETS AND TIES, SEATED
AROUND THE TABLE.

CAIAPHAS

How fares our prisoner, now?

SADOC

Why, the guards are having their way with him.

AMON

And the servants.

AZOR

Some of our fellow elders have taken to mocking him.

SADOC

No sleep this night for the pseudo Messiah!..

CAIAPHAS

Good. Very good.

JORAM

And what of the morrow?

AZOR

We will seek the sanction of Pontius Pilate.

AMON

And if it is not forthcoming?

CAIAPHAS

We will be there to make sure - secure a conviction.

AZOR

'Can be done, can be done.

SADOC

'Get the crowds on our side.

AMON

Sway them, persuade them.

CAIAPHAS

They'll follow if we lead.

JORAM

And what of the Procurator? What if he says no?

AZOR

'Not his own Master.

AMON

'Has to answer to Rome.

AZOR :

We'll play on that.

CAIAPHAS

'Watch him, intently. Search for a weakness... And if all comes to all, we'll threaten him.

JORAM

Caiaphas?

CAIAPHAS

'Say we will go over his head - if needs be, all the way to Rome...

SADOC

Ah-hh! Caiaphas is wise, wise!..

JORAM

Oh-hh... There's a thing...

CAIAPHAS

What?.. Joram?

JORAM

'But only now occurs to me... Is it not the custom at the Feast for the Procurator to release a prisoner?

SADOC

Why, so it is. I had forgotten.

CAIAPHAS

So?..

JORAM

Well... What if Pilate finds in favour of the Galilean, seeks to release him?

AZOR

'Invokes the custom?

SADOC

Jesus would walk free and all our efforts would be to no avail.

CAIAPHAS

Hmmm... For this, we must all be grateful to Rabbi Joram.

MURMURING... ASSENT.

SADOC

Then what to do? How avert this danger should it arise?..

CAIAPHAS

Do we know what felons are in the dungeons beneath the Praetorium... awaiting execution?

SADOC

Thieves, no doubt. Brigands. Robbers. The usual...

JORAM

And there is one in chains who was a danger to us all.

CAIAPHAS

Who?

JORAM

The Zealot. Jesus, son of Abbas.

AMON

Barabbas.

CAIAPHAS

That fellow... He still lives?

JORAM

To my certain knowledge, yes. 'Sentenced but not yet -

CAIAPHAS

Then... then let him be the one.

SADOC

High Priest?

CAIAPHAS

Should, perchance, the Procurator make to release the Nazarene, we will cry out for Barabbas.

AMON

Bar-Barabbas?..

JORAM

But - but he is a murderer?

CAIAPHAS

No matter, that. Don't you see? Barabbas led his rebels against the Eagles and was put down without mercy. If we favour him as against the Nazarene, it will be an insult to the very Emperor!..

MURMURING... ASSENT.

SADOC

Oh, marvel at the wisdom of our High Priest! -

AMON

Why, yes, of course! Now I -

CAIPHAS :

Then pass the word among our colleagues : "Not this man, but Barabbas!"

Let that be our cry! And I promise you, if we persist, calling again and again for the release of the Zealot, the people will follow suit!

AMON

Indeed, yes! Why, we could move among them -

AZOR

A Rabbi here, a scribe there -

SADOC

Calling with one voice for the release of Barabbas -

AZOR

Screaming for the blood of Jesus! -

CAIAPHAS

Threatening Caesar's envoy! -

SADOC

And the Romans cannot but buckle under such pressure!..

CAIAPHAS

Oh, my Rabbis! This coming day we will have our way with Pontius Pilate!..

DARKEN SET.

SCENE TWELVE

LIGHT THE CONFERENCE ROOM. CAIPHAS, AMON AND SADOC.

SADOC

See, High Priest. The night is fading. 'Time to make our move. Soon now... soon.

CAIAPHAS

We have gone over it, again and again, leaving nothing to –

ENTER AZOR AND JORAM.

Ah, Azor. Joram. What news?

AZOR

We have just learnt, High Priest, that a Galilean -

JORAM

One of the Twelve -

AZOR

Was but a while ago without in the Courtyard!

RHUBARB... DISBELIEF.

CAIAPHAS

What!? -

SADOC

But how - ?..

AZOR

We know not, Caiaphas.

AMON

'May have slipped past the Guard in the earlier confusion?

CAIAPHAS

Where is he now?

JORAM

Gone. Fled.

AZOR

One of the maid servants noticed him in the shadows -

JORAM

Put it to him that he was a Galilean, a follower of Jesus -

AZOR

Why, his very accent betrayed him.

CAIAPHAS

So?

JORAM

He swore he knew not the man, vehemently -

AZOR

And with much cursing and posturing -

JORAM

Thrice it was put to him -

AZOR

And thrice he protested, vigorously...

JORAM

And then he hurried out through the gates -

AZOR

Even as the dawn broke... and the cock crowed.

JORAM

A bystander who witnessed it came to us, aside -

AZOR

He recognised this Galilean as the one they call Peter -

JORAM

A fisherman. 'Seems he was very close to Jesus -

AZOR

A spokesperson of sorts for the others...

AMON

And the guards made no attempt to take him?

JORAM

They deemed him harmless -

AZOR

A blubber of fat and of no consequence -

JORAM

A fellow of nauseous cowardice...

MURMURING... RHUBARB.

CAIPHAS :

Oh, what kind of man do we hold in chains!

What manner of Messiah is this?!..

Look you:

this, this pretender consorts with whores,

publicans, sinners.

One of his so-called Twelve is a tax collector,

in the pay of Rome.

Another sells him for thirty pieces of silver -

the price of a slave.

And but now the eldest among them -

the fisherman who speaks for the others -

denies allegiance to him three times

when confronted by a mere maid servant!..

Dare anyone tell me this Jesus is the Messiah!?..

MURMURING... RHUBARB.

ENTER JUDAS, HOLDING A PURSE. THEIR OUTCRY:

AZOR

Iscariot! I do not believe - !

AMON

Judas? Here? But how? -

JORAM

How did he get past the Guard? -

AZOR

Someone will pay for this -

SADOC

Dearly -

CAIPHAS

Silence!..　　　You!.. Come forward...

JUDAS MOVES TOWARDS THEM... STOPS.

Yes?.. (PAUSE)   What is it?

JUDAS

I, I come to return your bribe...

AZOR

What?

SADOC

What are you - ?!..

JUDAS

I, I have sinned in betraying the blood of an innocent man...

AMON

Innocent? Huh! -

AZOR

Innocent, indeed!...

CAIAPHAS

What is that to us? It concerns you only...

JUDAS

You will take back the money you paid me.

CAIPHAS

No, we will not!

JUDAS

But you must...

CAIAPHAS

To what purpose? 'Alleviate your conscience?..

JUDAS

Please, I -

CAIAPHAS

No...

JUDAS

I, I beg you -

CAIAPHAS

No!..

JUDAS

Then, then I will return it from whence it came - to the Temple!

SADOC

The Temple?

JUDAS

Is it not from your coffers?

Donations of the poor,

offerings of worshippers,

the pence of the common people?..

You will find your silver on the floor of the Inner Sanctum!..

And may you all be damned - as I am!..

JUDAS HURRIES AWAY...

PAUSE.

SADOC

Well... What to make of that?

JORAM

Why such remorse?..

CAIAPHAS

No matter, that... Azor?

AZOR

Yes?

CAIAPHAS

Have a servant follow him. One you can truly trust. If Iscariot does as he so threatens, bid him gather up the coins -

AZOR

And return them to the coffers?

CAIAPHAS

No. Such monies must not be put in the Treasury.

JORAM

'Against the Law. It is the price of blood.

AMON

It would be a desecration.

SADOC

Well, then..?

CAIAPHAS

Let him come back here. We'll think of something...

AZOR NODS/SALUTES... EXITS.

PAUSE.

AMON

What to do? How go about disposing of blood money?..

SADOC

 Is there a precedent by which we may be guided?..

JORAM

Eh-hh... We have long been in need of a burial place for strangers.

CAIAPHAS

That's it! The very thing!..

AMON

The potter's field is there for the asking!

SADOC

'Could be ours for thirty pieces of silver!

CAIPHAS

Ah, ha! Why not? And no one need ever know!

JORAM

'This way, there is no sacrilege!

AMON

Much less blasphemy!..

CAIPHAS

Well, then... Sadoc, you hold the purse strings. See to it... And put my seal on the bill of sale.

SADOC :

The seal of the High Priest. Amen to that...

MURMURING... ASSENT, APPROVAL.

DARKEN SET.

SCENE THIRTEEN

LIGHT MAIN AREA. AZOR HAS AGAIN JOINED CAIPHAS, AMON, SADOC AND JORAM.

CAIAPHAS

See... The hour is upon us. 'Time to arraign our prisoner before the Governor - as a common criminal...

SADOC

Worse than any criminal - he is, in truth, a blasphemer!

CAIAPHAS

Indeed and indeed, Sadoc. Yet heed me well, my Rabbis - once at the gates of the Roman fortress, let there be no further mention of blasphemy.

AMON

What?

CAIAPHAS

Such an accusation could well rebound on us. In Roman law, blasphemy is of little consequence.

JORAM

Indeed...

CAIAPHAS

No, our brief must be more to the point - we will accuse the Galilean of most pernicious sedition -

AMON

Usurper of the peace! -

208

SADOC

Leading the people astray! -

AZOR

Inciting them to revolt and rebellion - against Rome! -

AMON

King! His claim to be King! -

CAIAPHAS

That above all! King of the Jews! In blatant contravention of the Emperor's august prerogative!.. But no mention of blasphemy. None. Are we agreed?

AGAIN ASSENT... APPROVAL.

This day we must prove ourselves to be true sons of the Most High! Men of Israel - and not mere vessels of clay!.. Let us arm ourselves, not with swords and cudgels, but with the words of the Sacred Scrolls burning on our lips, in our hearts:

CAIPHAS HAS PICKED UP A PAPER/DOCUMENT. HE READS :

"...You are not to listen to that prophet
or to the dreams of that dreamer...
That prophet or that dreamer of dreams
must be put to death,
for he has preached apostasy
from Yahweh your God...

You must banish this evil

from among you..."

JORAM

Deuteronomy -

CAIAPHAS

Correct. And let us not deviate, not for a moment, from those words
of wisdom!

ASSENT, APPROVAL.

Once on the cross, we will know - know beyond the shadow of a
doubt - that the Nazarene is a sham, fake, trickster. It is written:

"For one who has been hanged is accursed of God."

JORAM

Again, Deuteronomy - twenty one, if I am not mistaken.

CAIAPHAS

Precisely. You are well versed, Joram, in the scrolls of the
Pentateuch.

ENTER OFFICER.

JORAM

I thank you, Chief Rabbi. But I should also like to point out that -

CAIAPHAS

Ah-hh... Officer...

OFFICER

As you instructed, Rabbi, I have moved the prisoner into the
Courtyard.

CAIAPHAS

Good.

OFFICER

He stands there, bound and under guard.

CAIAPHAS

How is he now?

OFFICER

'Bloodied, his face swollen.

CAIAPHAS

Indeed... Then prepare to move him out.

OFFICER

And my orders?

CAIAPHAS

You will lead him to the Praetorium. I and my Sanhedrin will be
hard on your heels. Once there he is to be handed over to the
Romans. Do it - now.

THE OFFICER SALUTES, EXITS ON:

                                         Sir...

THEY STAND, SLIPPING ON THEIR JACKETS...

CAIAPHAS :

All the better that he is bloodied, bruised...

SADOC

Caiaphas?

CAIAPHAS :

Why, if he looks like a criminal the Romans may be persuaded - all the more easily - that he is a criminal...

MURMURING... SARDONIC LAUGHTER...

Joram?.. You were about to make a point, were you not?

JORAM

Eh-hh... 'Twas nothing, High Priest. Of, of no great import.

CAIAPHAS :

Well, then... Let us away! To the Praetorium!

ALL :

To the Praetorium!

CAIAPHAS :

Where we shall press our case on the Coloniser!..

THEY GATHER UP PAPERS, DOCUMENTS, BRIEF CASES... PUSH BACK CHAIRS... EXEUNT, AD-LIBBING...

JORAM STANDS... PONDERING... HESITANT... THEN HE, TOO, SHRUGS... EXITS...

END OF ACT ONE

ACT TWO

SCENE FOURTEEN

THE SET IN DARKNESS. LIGHT CAIPHAS AS HE ENTERS TO ONE SIDE, BEGINS TO MOVE THROUGH THE AUDITORIUM AND UNTO THE STAGE.

CAIAPHAS

Jesus, huh... Jesus.

From Galilee, eh?.. To the North... Galilee of the Gentiles...

Well, as we in the Sanhedrin well know, Galilee does not breed prophets!.. Huh. Does anything good - has ever anything good - come out of Galilee?..

Jesus! 'Had the sheer audacity to come among us, preaching to the people - our people - even in the very Temple. Doing so-called good works. Claiming - how dare he! - to be the son of the Most High!..

Too far! 'Went far too far!..

Drawing the people away from us,

tripping us up in open debate!

Insulting - scorning - castigating us - publicly!..

Such searing embarrassment, abject humiliation!..

Well, enough is enough - we nailed the son of a bitch!..

Dead, now.

Dead and buried.

Over.

Done with.

Finished...

And I, Caiaphas, Chief Rabbi and High Priest of Israel,

was to the fore in tracking, hounding, bringing him down...

SCENE FIFTEEN

LIGHT THE CONFERENCE ROOM AS HE CROSSES, SEATS
HIMSELF AT THE "TOP OF THE TABLE," BEGINS TO SIFT
THROUGH PAPERS, DOCUMENTS...
ENTER AMON.

CAIAPHAS

Ah, Rabbi Amon. Peace be with you.

AMON

And with you, High Priest.

CAIAPHAS

I trust you slept well?

AMON

The sleep of the just, Caiaphas. To be candid, I was quite spent.

CAIAPHAS

As were we all, Amon - all of us in the Sanhedrin. What! A day and
a night and the following day without sleep?

AMON

Well worth it - worth every strenuous moment of it. To have done
with the Nazarene - and forever!

CAIAPHAS

But a few days from now it will be as if he never existed...

As near to annihilation as we could come - within the Law.

AMON

The people will turn back to us now. All will be as it was.

CAIAPHAS

It was either him or us - no middle ground...

AMON

And his followers gone into hiding. In fear for their lives.

CAIAPHAS

Leave them be. They will disperse by and by, return to Galilee.

Without their leader they are headless chickens...

AMON

And that will be the end of it.

CAIAPHAS

Hmmm... Are the others up and about - Sadoc, Azor?..

AMON

Perhaps. I have not -

CAIAPHAS

Go, summon them, Amon. I have in mind a brief conference... Let us

be on guard still a while. Did he not say that within three days he

would rise again?

AMON

The ranting of a mad man!..

CAIAPHAS

Quite. And yet there could be a ruse here we cannot foresee. We

must needs be wary...

FADE LIGHTS AS AMON TURNS, EXITS...

SCENE SIXTEEN

LIGHT ROOM TO REVEAL JORAM SEATED AT A P.C.,
TAPPING THE KEYS, OBSERVING THE SCREEN...

AMON ENTERS, STOPS SHORT WHEN HE SEES JORAM.

AMON

Joram?.. Joram!

JORAM

Wh-what?

AMON

What, indeed! The High Priest has called a meeting of the Inner
Circle and you sit there, this hour of the morning, scrolling!

JORAM

Well, I, I -

AMON

Sadoc, Azor and the others - are they up and about?

JORAM

Eh, I - I have no idea.

AMON

Then come! Let us summon them!

JORAM

Eh, quite. If, if you will bear with me a moment...

JORAM TURNS TO THE PC, SCRIBBLES A NOTE...

Twenty two... Eli, eli, lama... sab... achthani...

AMON

What?

JORAM

What he said - cried out from the cross - the Nazarene. I've searched
back, traced it to source -

AMON

Oh, in the name of the All Holy! What ails you, Rabbi? The wretch
was in fever - delirious! 'Screaming we know not what! Some of us
reckoned he was calling on one of the prophets -

JORAM

No. Not so -

AMON

And a lewd fellow broke from the crowd... ran forward... offered
him a sponge of vinegar. He tasted it and, and died.

JORAM

But not before he signalled a psalm - knowing that sooner or later we
would source it.

AMON

What? -

JORAM

He was not calling on Elias or any of the prophets. See for yourself.

AMON HESITATES, THEN CROSSES RELUCTANTLY TO THE
PC, LEANS FORWARD, SURVEYS THE SCREEN.

The twenty second psalm of David - 'very first line:

———

218

"My God, my God, why hast thou forsaken me?.."

AMON

Huh. Hmmm... So... if it be true - if these are the words he -

JORAM

'No doubt about it -

AMON

Then be it so. 'An apt choice of Scripture for a man in darkest despair.

JORAM

If so he was.

AMON

What?!..

JORAM :

There's more... Look, Rabbi. See, I have high-lighted some of...

My throat is dried up like baked clay...
my tongue cleaves to my jaws...
They divide my garments among them
 and for my raiment they cast lots...

AMON TURNS AWAY, AGITATED, AS JORAM CONTINUES:

For my thirst they gave me vinegar to drink...
My friends and companions shun me...

AMON   (TURNING BACK)

Enough!

JORAM

I am a worm and no man...

All who see me sneer at me,

they toss their heads and sneer -

AMON

Enough, Joram! That will be quite enough!

Switch that damned thing off! Do it!

JORAM SHRUGS, LEANS FORWARD, SWITCHES OFF THE
PC.

JORAM

Did it happen, Amon, but yesterday? To the letter? This prediction

of David - fulfilled to the letter? -

AMON

Oh, what insanity is this?! You are mad to tinker with the scrolls

thus! I, too, can quote chapter and verse - readily vouch for a

contradictory thesis! You tamper at your peril with the express will

of the Sanhedrin!

JORAM

But I -

AMON   (TURNING AWAY)

Now, come! Enough of digressions! The High Priest awaits us...

JORAM

Amon?..

AMON STOPS, TURNS BACK.

220

Psalm twenty two ends on a high note - victory, triumph for the Most High.

AMON

Take care, Rabbi. Take great care.

JORAM

You will report me?

AMON

You leave me no choice...

AMON TURNS, EXITS.

JORAM STANDS, PONDERING.

DARKEN THE SET.

SCENE SEVENTEEN

LIGHT THE CONFERENCE ROOM. CAIPHAS IN SITU.

ENTER SADOC AND AZOR. THEY SEAT THEMSELVES, SPREAD PAPERS, UNZIP BRIEF CASES, ETC.

ENTER AMON. HE GOES DIRECTLY TO CAIPHAS, LEANS DOWN, WHISPERS IN HIS EAR... CAIPHAS FROWNS.

AMON TURNS AWAY AS JORAM ENTERS, SEATS HIMSELF...

CAIAPHAS
So... all here, then?
SADOC
A full quorum, Caiaphas.
CAIAPHAS
Then let us proceed... I know how you wish it was over, done with. But we must steel ourselves, remain vigilant, see this through to the very end. Otherwise his followers - the rabble from Galilee - may still upstage us.

RHUBARB... MURMURING OF ASSENT...

For posterity, then, let the minutes show - recorded as diligently as ever by our assiduous Sadoc -

SADOC

You are too kind, High Priest -

CAIAPHAS

That we witnessed this fellow's crucifixion.

AMON

Just so -

CAIAPHAS

And his death.

SADOC

Without a doubt, High Priest.

AMON

We can vouch for it. He was dead before he was taken down.

JORAM

Why, one of the soldiers ran a spear through his side - there came
out blood and water.

CAIAPHAS

Mmmm... So then?..

SADOC

Eh-hh... It seems that Joseph of Arimathea -

CAIAPHAS

Seems, Sadoc? Seems?! Let us have facts!

SADOC TAKEN ABACK... THEN RECOVERING...

SADOC

Well... the fact is, Joseph of Arimathea went directly to the Roman
Governor, obtained permission to bury the Galilean -

AMON

We were still there on Golgotha when he returned -

SADOC

Hurrying. Out of breath.

AMON

The mercenaries helped to draw the nails -

JORAM

Lower the body to the ground...

AMON

His mother was at hand. As were some of his followers.

CAIAPHAS

Oh, please - spare me... So - then?

JORAM

Why, they wrapped the corpse in clean linen -

AZOR

Clean linen?!

SADOC

That was his doing - Jo-Joseph of -

CAIAPHAS

Go on.

AMON

And they carried the remains to a tomb -

SADOC

A new grave this Joseph had nominated - and laid it against the back
wall.

CAIAPHAS

You saw? Witnessed?

AMON

On my oath, High Priest -

JORAM

'As near as I now am to you, Caiaphas.

CAIAPHAS

And?..

SADOC :

Then they emerged and fell to pushing a great stone across the entrance -

AMON

To seal it.

CAIAPHAS

They?

JORAM

Joseph and some of his ilk -

SADOC

Nor were we the only witnesses.

CAIAPHAS

Oh?..

AMON

His mother was close by -

JORAM

With some other Galileans. Women for the most part...

AMON

So we waited a while longer -

JORAM

Until near dusk. The Sabbath was upon us –

SADOC

Then we turned away, returned to Jerusalem...

CAIAPHAS

We are agreed, then: he died and was buried?..

RHURBARB... ASSENT...

So... who minds the tomb now?

AMON

Why... Well, no one, to our knowledge...

CAIAPHAS

Then... then what is there to stop his followers rolling back the stone, stealing away the corpse - then spreading a rumour, starting a subterfuge, perhaps even initiating a cult?..

MURMURING

Sadoc?

SADOC

High Priest?

CAIAPHAS

You will go at once to the Praetorium. Amon and Azor to go with you. Once there demand - I say, demand - an audience with the Procurator.

SADOC

But - but it is the Sabbath. We are forbidden to set foot on pagan soil.

CAIAPHAS

Then bid him meet you at the main gates.

You will put to him our fear of espionage - a Galilean conspiracy -
press him to mount a guard at the tomb.

AMON

Ah! How very - !

MURMURING ASSENT

CAIAPHAS

Now go - hurry!

SADOC, AZOR AND AMON EXEUNT, AD-LIBBING...
JORAM RISES, MAKES TO FOLLOW THEM.

JORAM

I, too, will go -

CAIAPHAS

No. No, I think not. No need. They are well able to do my bidding...
Let you and I parley a while... Rabbi Joram.

JORAM SEATS HIMSELF AGAIN. HE IS APPREHENSIVE.

So... you have been scrolling?..

JORAM

Eh-hh... A little, yes. Here and there. A snatch of research - no more.

CAIAPHAS

And what have you uncovered?

JORAM

Oh-hh... Nothing of any great significance -

CAIAPHAS

Oh, Rabbi, Rabbi! Would you dabble with the truth, deceive your High Priest?

JORAM :

Eh-hh... I, eh -

CAIAPHAS

Tell me.

JORAM

Well, though we were not there on the Mount of Olives, did not actually witness the capture of Jesus in the Garden of Gethsemani -

CAIAPHAS

Indeed -

JORAM

We have the assurance of the Temple militia that his closest followers abandoned him and, and fled.

CAIAPHAS

Agreed.

JORAM

The Iscariot returned here as he had gone out - with the Temple Guard. Intent on securing our bribe.

CAIAPHAS

To the point, Joram! To the point!

JORAM TAKES A PAPER/DOCUMENT FROM A JACKET POCKET.

JORAM

I - I have found a passage in Zecharias that is uncannily close to the mark.

CAIAPHAS

Oh?

JORAM (READING)

Thirteen, seven. *"I will smite the shepherd, and the sheep of the flock will be scattered..."*

CAIPHAS

And?.. So?

JORAM :

Well, do you not think - I mean, is it not incredibly akin to the fulfilment of a, a - ?

CAIPHAS

Prophesy?.. Zecharias is, after all, one of our revered prophets.

JORAM

In-incredible as it may seem?..

CAIPHAS

(STANDING, CIRCLING)

No. No, I think not... Unless - unless suddenly - overnight - by some kind of Divine intervention -

JORAM

High Priest?

CAIPHAS

A carpenter from Nazareth becomes a shepherd!..   (PAUSE)

You sit there and tell me all that befell the Nazarene on the Mount of Olives was in fulfillment of a prophesy?!

JORAM

Well, I, I -

CAIAPHAS

Oh, Rabbi! Rabbi Joram! 'Easy enough to cull through the prophesies of yore - deleting here, high-lighting there - 'come to a conclusion far removed from Orthodoxy!

JORAM

Still, it would seem on the face of it -

CAIAPHAS

On the face of it? On the face of it?!.. Now hear me, Joram, mark well my words! Abide by the counsel of your fellow Scribes - settle for the collective wisdom of the Sanhedrin - and you will not - cannot - falter!..

JORAM

Yes, I -

CAIAPHAS

As if I did not have enough to engage me without one of my Inner Circle scrolling, amiss, the Scriptures... Now leave me. Keep to yourself a while. I will expect you back here when the others return from the Praetorium.

JORAM

As you wish...

JORAM STANDS... PREPARES TO EXIT.

CAIAPHAS :

Oh, and Joram?..

JORAM TURNS, HESITATES. CAIPHAS CONSULTS A
DOCUMENT.

You like it here, do you not?

JORAM

High Priest?

CAIAPHAS

Jerusalem. The Temple. Your work with the people..?

JORAM

Indeed. Very much so.

CAIAPHAS

Hmmm... I should tell you that one of our brethren has gone to his
rest. Recently. 'A town out in the country - if it can be called a town.
'Desolate, by all accounts. Still... the synagogue there is now in need
of a Rabbi. It is for me to decide on a replacement. Soon... You
understand?..

JORAM STANDS A MOMENT, THEY LOOK AT EACH
OTHER.
THEN JORAM NODS... TURNS... EXITS.
DARKEN THE CONFERENCE ROOM.

SCENE EIGHTEEN

LIGHT THE CONFERENCE ROOM AS SADOC, AMON AND AZOR ENTER IN HIGH DUDGEON...

SADOC

How dare he! Dismiss us with such arrogance!..

AMON

Roman imperialist! -

AZOR

Foul foreigner!..

SADOC

No concept of our righteousness! -

AMON

And what is more, kept us waiting! Why, I had a mind to - !

ENTER CAIAPHAS. HE SURVEYS THEM AS THEY SUBSIDE.

SADOC

Enough, Amon -

AMON

What?.. Oh-hh...

CAIAPHAS SEATS HIMSELF AT THE TOP OF THE TABLE, GESTURES TO THEM TO BE SEATED. THEY DO SO...

CAIAPHAS

So..?

SADOC

We, we went as you bade us, High Priest - to, to the Praetorium -

AZOR

To the gates. Only as far as the main entrance -

AMON

And when he came down - after some time, some considerable time
- Pilate, that is - he was none too pleased at our request -

SADOC

Oh, quite the Imperial pagan -

JORAM ENTERS, SEATS HIMSELF AT THE END TABLE.

AZOR

Put us down, out of hand -

AMON

Oh, what contempt - as though we were fools, imbeciles! -

SADOC

"Send Roman mercenaries to mount a guard at the tomb of a dead
man? How very absurd!"

AZOR

"You have your own guards. See to it yourselves!"

SADOC

Those were his very words, High Priest -

AMON

And none other did he speak. 'Turned and went back in...

CAIPHAS

Hmmm... And yet... in his very arrogance he has played into our hands...

JORAM

What? How do you - ?

SADOC

Caiaphas?..

CAIAPHAS

He has sanctioned the deployment of the Sanhedrin's militia, has he not?

AZOR

So?

CAIPHAS

They will be on our side, their allegiance assured.

AMON

Ah, yes! Yes, indeed! -

SADOC

No truck with Roman mercenaries!..

CAIAPHAS

Joram...

JORAM

High Priest?

CAIAPHAS :

You know well the Guards of the Temple -

better than any of us.

JORAM

Well, I -

CAIPHAS

Then choose among them - guards you would trust with your life.
Have two of them go at once to mount the first watch. Relieve them
every six hours.

JORAM STANDS, MAKES TO LEAVE...

Better still, you yourself will lead them to the tomb - lest they, by
some mishap, mistake it.

JORAM   (GOING)

As you wish...

CAIAPHAS

Oh, and Joram?

JORAM   (TURNING BACK)

Yes?

CAIPHAS

The great stone at the entrance to the tomb - have them put a seal on
it.

EXIT JORAM. THE OTHERS AD-LIB THEIR APPROVAL...

Oh, Caiaphas... how very wise!..

Indeed... indeed...

Well said, High Priest...

DARKEN THE CONFERENCE ROOM.

SCENE NINETEEN

LIGHT THE CONFERENCE ROOM. CAIAPHAS AND THE OTHERS - EXCEPT JORAM - SEATED AROUND THE TABLE, AS BEFORE. RHUBARB...

AMON

... He's out there somewhere. Now a free man...

SADOC

Who?

AMON

Barabbas.

AZOR

So?

AMON

Well... it is we who won him his freedom.

CAIAPHAS

And?.. What of it?

AMON

We... yesterday we watched as he emerged from the dungeons, unshackled... supported by Roman guards... a weakling, blinded, blinking in the sudden sun -

CAIAPHAS

To the point, Amon! To the point!

AMON

Well, what when the days pass and he recovers his strength? Will the

Zealots gather round him? Will he return to robbery? Turn again to the trade routes? Pillage and plunder the caravans? Round, once more, on the Occupiers?

AZOR

And what if he does?

AMON

Will the blame be laid at our door?..

CAIAPHAS

No matter that. It will have been well worth the risk.

AZOR

Why, look what we have achieved, Amon!

SADOC

How else could we have turned the tables on the Procurator?

CAIAPHAS

And if Barabbas does as you say - turns again to his old ways - it will be for the Romans to deal with him.

AZOR

Wisely, we will distance ourselves.

SADOC

But of course! We should have nothing to do with murder and revolt!

AZOR

It is not in our brief. Not our vocation.

CAIAPHAS

Why, look you, my Rabbis: if we are not custodians of the scrolls, keepers of the Law and the Peace that flows from the exact observance of the Law - what are we?..

RHUBARB OF APPROVAL... JORAM ENTERS, JOINS THEM...

Ah, Joram... All in order?

JORAM

Indeed, High Priest. The first watch is now mounted -

CAIAPHAS

Good. Very good -

JORAM

The tomb sealed. And I have assigned the two most reliable guards of the Temple to keep vigil from midnight until daybreak.

CAIAPHAS

Excellent!

JORAM

I thank you, High Priest.

CAIPHAS

All we can now do is wait. And pray.

SADOC

Pray?

CAIAPHAS :

That Jesus is in that pit of Hell reserved for blasphemers - from whence there is no return...

APPROVAL, ASSENT...
ENTER SERVANT.

CAIAPHAS   (CALLING)
Yes, what is it?

SERVANT

One, one of the other servants on, on her way here just now -

CAIAPHAS

What about her?

SERVANT

She, she came upon the lifeless body of Judas. Judas Iscariot.

SADOC

Oh!?..

SERVANT

Hanging from a tree in the Cedron Valley.

CAIAPHAS :

I see... Very well. You may go.   (EXIT SERVANT)

SADOC

Hanged himself?..

CAIAPHAS

So? What is it to us? He was useful, to a point. Once the Galilean was ours, he was expendable...

AZOR

This is indeed good news.

AMON

He is muted now - by his own hand.

SADOC

But of course! He can no longer bear witness to our bribery!

AZOR

Our thirty pieces of silver will remain a secret for all time - all time!

CAIAPHAS :

And so - to Perdition with him!

ASSENT... CAIAPHAS STANDS, THEY FOLLOW SUIT.

Come. The day is done, nightfall is upon us. Let us to our rest,

Rabbis...

SADOC

A fresh start begins on the morrow -

AZOR

Mark my words, High Priest - the dawn will bring your day of days!

CAIAPHAS

Well... we shall see.

AZOR

Oh, Caiaphas, Caiaphas! Why do you fret so? Not even the very

Prophets of old were able to come back from the dead! -

AMON

What chance, then, a convicted blasphemer - ?

SADOC

A carpenter's son from Galilee - ?

AMON

A shyster from Nazareth - ?..

RHUBARB... DARKEN THE CONFERENCE ROOM.

SCENE TWENTY

LIGHT THE CONFERENCE ROOM. THE GANG OF FIVE
ASSEMBLING...

AZOR

So... the hours of darkness - and danger - are now behind us -

SADOC

The sun shines on Jerusalem - and on the House of our High Priest! -

AMON

The Sabbath come and gone - and nothing awry! -

JORAM

No attempt made on the Tomb! -

AZOR

No sighting of the Galileans! -

SADOC

The danger has passed, High Priest - we have won!

VICTORIOUS RHUBARB.

A few days from now the Nazarene will be but a faded memory, his
corpse rotten in an unmarked grave!

AMON

I say it out, my friends - this day marks an end - and a new
beginning!..

CAIAPHAS

Hear me, my elders! Hear me!..

RHUBARB SUBDUED TO EXPECTANT QUIET.

CAIAPHAS

My scribes, elders, fellow Rabbis... I counsel caution... There will be a time for celebration by and by... The third day has only just begun. Until the sun sets on our Holy City we must take every precau -

ENTER AN AGITATED SERVANT.

Yes? What is it?

SERVANT

Two, two of the Temple guards, High Priest, are without -

CAIAPHAS

So?

SERVANT

They have come in haste from the tomb -

CAIAPHAS

And?

SERVANT

They are much put out, request a meeting with Rabbi Joram, urgently.

JORAM :

Oh. I will go out to -

CAIAPHAS

No! If there is something amiss here, we ought all - Show them in!

EXIT SERVANT.

MURMURING... ILL AT EASE...

SADOC

What can it be? -

AZOR

Some trickery, perhaps? -

JORAM

Are we to be trumped? -

ENTER TWO GUARDS. THEY HANG BACK...

Oh!.. Oh-hh... These are the two I chose to... Come forward! Zach...
Achim... Be not afraid...

THE GUARDS MOVE INTO THE ROOM, RELUCTANTLY.

CAIAPHAS

So... Tell me, why are you distressed, so on edge?..

ACHIM

The, the tomb... Jesus of... The, the Nazarene -

ZACH

Achim? Say it, Achim -

CAIAPHAS

Come, speak up, man! What about the tomb?

ACHIM

It - it is open. Empty. The body is, is gone...

ZACH

Not there. Not any more -

SILENCE... THEN RHUBARB, CONSTERNATION

SADOC

What gibberish is this! -

JORAM

I trusted you both! -

AMON

What say you, soldier? -

CAIAPHAS

Quiet! Quiet, I say!..

RHUBARB SUBSIDING...

Let them speak - and without interruption... Now... Achim. Zach...
You will tell us precisely and in exact detail what happened. And
how... I am waiting.

ACHIM

We - we were but a while ago at the rock, guarding the tomb -

CAIAPHAS

That we know. So?

ACHIM

And the sun, sun had begun to rise -

ZACH

Dawn light -

ACHIM

When two women drew near -

ZACH

Mary of Magdala and another we did not recognise...

CAIAPHAS

Yes?

ACHIM

We, we challenged them - as we were in duty bound -

ZACH

'Called to them to keep their distance -

ACHIM

And even as they halted, there was a, a clap of thunder -

SADOC

What! There was no thunder, you dolt! It is a pleasant morning! -

CAIAPHAS

Silence! Hear them out!.. Continue.

ACHIM

And then, this - this man - this creature - appeared before us...

CAIAPHAS

Appeared?..

ZACH

I, I looked up and he was suddenly there - come from nowhere!..

CAIAPHAS

Describe him.

ACHIM

Why, his, his face shone like lightning -

ZACH

And his garments were, were white as snow...

RHURBARB... INCREDULITY.

CAIAPHAS

Quiet!.. I will hear them, unhampered!.. So... An angel. What else
but an angel?

ACHIM

I, I was afraid to say so...

CAIAPHAS

Afraid of incurring our wrath... And tell me, my soldiers - were you
afraid of this, this apparition?

ZACH

We were in awe, overcome -

ACHIM

Stricken to the ground -

ZACH

Weak we were, as if in fever -

ACHIM

Our weapons useless...

CAIAPHAS

And then?..

ACHIM

He, he moved the rock aside -

CAIAPHAS

What?! -

ZACH

As though it were feather-light...

ACHIM

And he, he sat on it.

INCREDULITY...

CAIAPHAS

An angel who sits on a stone. Hmmm... Did he speak?

ZACH

Not to us -

ZACH

To the women -

SADOC

Are we expected to stand here and listen to this, this -

AMON

Nonsense! -

CAIAPHAS

Hear them, I pray you, my Rabbis! Let us be patient a while longer...
So? What did he say to these women?..

ACHIM

'Told them that Jesus had risen -

ZACH

'Bade them enter the tomb, see for themselves -

CAIAPHAS

And they so did?

ACHIM

Yes - but fearfully. They remarked on the winding sheet, still there,
in which he had been buried -

ZACH

Blood stained...

SADOC   (EXPLODING)

Do you know what you are saying?! Men have been stoned to -

CAIAPHAS

Sadoc!.. For the last time! You will have your say bye and bye... So?

ZACH

So then he was gone -

ACHIM

As he had come - suddenly, out of nowhere...

CAIAPHAS

And the women?

ACHIM

They stepped out of the tomb and hurried away.

CAIAPHAS

Huh. Why the haste?

ZACH

He had given them a message for the, the Galileans...

CAIAPHAS

Yes?

ACHIM

They, they are to return to Galilee. There they will...

CAIAPHAS

What?

ACHIM

See him... See the Nazarene.

                    MURMURING... DISBELIEF...

CAIAPHAS

So... Even as we speak these women - Mary of Magdala and the nameless one - are on their way to Bethany.

AZOR

Bethany?

CAIAPHAS

I am reliably informed that a number of his followers are there and in hiding...

SADOC

This is all so-so - I am speechless.

CAIAPHAS

Good... Now we must put our heads together as never before. Joram?

JORAM

Rabbi?

CAIAPHAS

Confine these two stalwarts to the ante-room. They are to communicate with no one. You understand? No one.

JORAM

(TO THE GUARDS)

This way... Follow me...

CAIAPHAS

We will summon them when we have deliberated...

EXEUNT JORAM AND THE GUARDS.

AMON

What to make of it? -

AZOR

They seem sincere, worthy of our trust -

SADOC

Yet somehow – 'some way we know not - they have been beguiled -

AMON

But how was it devised - executed?..

CAIAPHAS

Oh, I feared something like this! But I knew not what - or from
whence it would come... And when word of it begins to spread..?
Then mark well my words - we must keep a common front on this,
hold the line, act as one...

RHUBARB OF ASSENT.

And pay a price - however great - to ensure our survival!

SADOC

Survival?

CAIAPHAS

If the people hear of this foul fiction, this cancerous rumour -

AZOR

They will turn away from us -

AMON

No. No, we must protect ourselves! -

SADOC

If we hold firm, keep our nerve, stand united -

AZOR

Though we may lose some ground to the Galileans -

AMON

Our ascendancy will still be assured -

SADOC

He died and was buried - and we will keep him that way!

AZOR

And if that means emptying the coffers?

AMON

Then we will do it - and be damned!

CAIAPHAS

We will most assuredly be damned if we do not... Sadoc.

SADOC

High Priest?

CAIPHAS

See to it. A price they cannot refuse... Let us finish this business as we began - with a bribe. One that will seal the lips of the guards for ever more...

EXIT SADOC AS THE OTHERS MURMUR IN ASSENT.

DARKEN ROOM.

SCENE TWENTY ONE

LIGHT THE CONFERENCE ROOM AS JORAM ENTERS, JOINS
AZOR, AMON AND CAIAPHAS AT THE CONFERENCE
TABLE.

CAIAPHAS

How are they now?

JORAM

'More, I think more at ease. I fetched them some food from the
kitchens -

CAIPHAS

Good. And no contact?

JORAM

No. None whatever.

CAIPHAS

Very good. Well, their confinement is nigh ended –

ENTER SADOC.
HE PLACES TWO "BAGS OF COINS" ON THE TABLE. HE IS
BREATHLESS, WINDED FROM HIS EXERTIONS.
MEANWHILE:

JORAM

But - but what if it be true?

AMON

What?

JORAM

What if, in truth, he has come back from the -

SADOC

Joram!

AZOR

You speak blasphemy!

AMON

Such treachery! And from a Rabbi!

CAIAPHAS

Ha! See! Even from beyond the grave the Nazarene infiltrates this
Assembly!

AMON

What?

CAIAPHAS

Sowing a doubt, starting a dispute, precipitating a split!..

SADOC

Split? In the Sanhedrin? Never!

AZOR

We cannot - must not - allow it!

AMON

Put it out of your mind, Joram! Exorcise this demon - once and for
all!

CAIAPHAS :

Oh, Joram, Joram! Are you, too, from Galilee?..

SADOC

What? A naked Messiah, crucified between two criminals!? Oh,
Rabbi Joram! The very thought is anathema! -

CAIAPHAS

'Goes against all the Messianic traditions we Jews hold so dearly! -

AZOR

'Have held down through the ages!

AMON

And will continue to cherish until the true Messiah comes in glory!..

SADOC

Then enough of rancour! Let us be as one -

CAIAPHAS

And are we as one about the way ahead?..

RHUBARB OF ASSENT.

And without dissension?.. Joram?

JORAM

I... I agree.

CAIAPAS

Good. Then call them. Let us get this done with.

JORAM STANDS, CROSSES... OPENS A DOOR, OFF...

CAIAPHAS

You were laden down, Sadoc?

SADOC

Indeed. Much more than thirty pieces of -

AMON

'Worth it if it buys their allegiance.

AZOR

They will not refuse such a sum - could not.

JORAM   (CALLING)

Guards?.. Enter. Come forward...

ACHIM AND ZACH ENTER, RELUCTANTLY... HESITANT.

Come... Come now... No need to be so... You have nothing to fear
from the High Priest... or any member of the Sanhedrin...

CAIAPHAS

Ah-hh... Guards... We are grateful to you for bearing with us, will
detain you no longer than is... We are aware how tired you must be...
Exhausted. It was a long night out there... And a cold one... A lesser
man - less disciplined soldier - could well have nodded off...
Indeed... Oh, and understandably so... And quite forgivable... Tell
me, did you nod off at any time?

ZACH

Eh-hh... towards dawn. I, I grew heavy-lidded - but Achim roused
me, brought me back to -

CAIAPHAS

There! See! Long hours, unending sentinel - and two soldiers who
are only human...

                    MURMURING

'Strikes me you both may have nodded off..?

ACHIM

What!? Well, no -

CAIPHAS

Indeed, that you fell into a heavy slumber..?

ZACH

No, not so! I can vouch for the fact that -

CAIAPHAS

Look you! Here! More money than you ever dreamt of...

ACHIM

I... Why, I -

CAIAPHAS

A bag for each of you...

ZACH

Oh. Oh, it... it -

CAIAPHAS

Yours. For the taking.

AMON

You will never want again -

AZOR

Go where you like, do as you wish -

SADOC

Assume, if needs be, a new identity -

AMON

Travel. The pleasures of the world, yours at will -

SADOC

And in return we ask for little enough -

CAIAPHAS

A simple story, straightforward - you gave way to tiredness.

You will say - under oath, if needs be - that while you slept thus -

the followers of the Nazarene came by stealth and stole away his body...

ZACH

But, but if the Governor should hear of our -

ACHIM

Yes, yes! If Pontius Pilate gets wind of -

CAIPHAS

Leave Rome to me! I will deal with the Procurator!.. I, Caiaphas, High Priest of Israel, give you my word. No harm will come to you.

AZOR

Well..? What is your response?

ZACH

I, I... Achim?..

AMON

It is a fortune!

AZOR

Silver. All silver.

SADOC

Well? Do we have your word? -

AMON

That what has been said will never pass beyond these walls?..

CAIAPHAS

Come! How say you?..

ACHIM

Eh-hh... I agree.

ZACH

And I... Yes, I -

CAIAPHAS

Good, very good...

(RHUBARB, APPROVAL.)

AZOR

Let them swear it, Caiaphas.

CAIAPHAS

Indeed. To seal the pact...

ACHIM

I, I swear. On my oath as a guard of the Temple -

ZACH

And on mine - as a soldier of the Sanhedrin, I, I swear.

CAIAPHAS

Then take it.

THE GUARDS STEP FORWARD, PICK UP THE BAGS.

Joram, see them out... Doubtless, they will sleep a while. And then...

JORAM

Then?

CAIAPHAS

Let them make a spirited start –

bear witness against the Galileans...

JORAM SEES "THEM OUT..."

AMON

Oh, well accomplished, High Priest!

CAIAPHAS

No joy for me, Amon. 'Had to be done.

AZOR

'Only way -

AMON

'Protect ourselves -

SADOC

Ensure our survival -

AZOR

A good morning's work -

AMON

We can only pray now - that our story sticks -

SADOC

'Go all the way on this one -

AMON

And we will, we will! -

AZOR

'Must! -

JORAM   (RETURNING)

If, if we are found out..? Exposed to the common people... As liars, deceivers, bribers -

CAIAPHAS

But do you not see? What we do is for the people! For their own very best good - protection! Else they could well be led astray by this, this fractious deceit!..

RHUBARB OF ASSENT... DYING DOWN FOR:

Oh, would that we could tell how it is in Bethany!..

SADOC

High Priest?

CAIAPHAS

There is the crucial issue... The witness of Magdalene and her friend - will it be believed or not?

AZOR

If not, if the Galileans dismiss their testimony - ?

CAIPHAS

Then we can sleep serenely in our beds... But who can say? They are gullible, these Galileans, prone to believe the unbelievable. After all, they believed in him when he lived, hung on his every word... Some of them may even now be hurrying back to the tomb to see for themselves. If they become convinced that he lives anew, has gone ahead of them to Galilee..?

AMON

Caiaphas?

CAIAPHAS

Then a myth is born. Oh, a monster...

JORAM

So?.. If our worst fears are realised?..

CAIAPHAS

They will wait until sunset, then begin the journey North in twos and threes under cover of darkness. Were I a Galilean, that would be my strategy.

AZOR

And once there?

CAIAPHAS

They will begin to sow this perfidious seed, spread this, this diabolical deceit. And a malignant cancer will have taken root in Judaism...

MURMURS OF DISMAY... DISBELIEF.

SADOC

But this is absurd! Where is the hard evidence? 'Empty tomb, empty tomb! Ha!.. The linen shroud he was wrapped in still there!.. So what wears he, this resurrection man? Has he perchance filched a tunic from a clothes-line?..

LAUGHTER.

Or perhaps he is given to nudity?

LOUDER LAUGHTER...

AZOR

Does he breathe, have a heart beat? Is there blood in his veins? If so, from whence does it come? He was bloodless when taken down from the cross was he not?

SADOC

Oh, it is so utterly preposterous! 'Foolish of us to dwell on it further.

AMON

No sign as yet of Judas Iscariot...

SADOC

What?

AMON

Has he not also risen from the dead? What could be keeping him?

LAUGHTER... DERISION.

AZOR

It may become the fashion. When Barabbas passes away the Zealots will surely claim for him immortality!

FURTHER DERISION...

CAIAPHAS

Oh, well you may laugh. And I would willingly laugh with you - were it not so serious an issue, so insidiously dangerous...
Look you, my Rabbis:
No one has ever come back from the dead.
No Jew, no gentile. No saint, sinner.
No prophet, hero, slave, emperor, king...
But now it is put to us that the leader
of a clandestine sect from the North
is back from beyond the grave!
Oh, what sheer piffle! What undiluted rubbish!

MURMURING ASSENT.

Are we not the custodians of the Law, the protectors of the Covenant?.. Then are we not duty-bound to attack this malignancy, destroy it before it takes root, begins to spread!..

SADOC

Oh, the wisdom of our High Priest! How say you, Caiaphas?..

CAIAPHAS

We will speak out in the name of Orthodoxy, in defence of the Law and the Prophets - all we hold dear!.. We will denounce this rabble in our synagogues, our public places, at every opportunity! Put them down, rout them, destroy their witness!

AZOR

Deny them entrance to our places of worship on the Sabbath!

AMON

That would most certainly grieve them -

SADOC

Cut them off! Bar them! Bring them to their senses!

CAIAPHAS

And we will hold fast by our strategy - they came by night and stole away his corpse.

AMON

What a stroke of good fortune...

SADOC

What?

AMON

That it was two of our Temple guards who were on duty at the tomb - and not Roman mercenaries.

MURMURING ASSENT.

CAIAPHAS

Believe me, if this schism takes root - if it is not stamped out - much harm will befall the Jews...

SADOC

It will be our word against theirs. That is the sum of it.

CAIAPHAS

Indeed. And may continue to be so - who knows? - down the generations...

JORAM

Yes, but if...

AZOR

What?

JORAM

If, as we maintain, the Galileans went by night - the hours of night that have but passed - and stole away his corpse, then why, why have the Magdalene and this other woman gone to Bethany with a contradictory witness?..

AMON

What?!..

FEMALES SCREAMING, SHRIEKING IN TERROR, OFF.

SADOC

What the - ?!

CAIAPHAS

Now what comes about? -

ENTER SERVANT, AGITATED...

What? What is it? -

SERVANT

It is the maid servants, High Priest!

CAIAPHAS

What about them?

SERVANT

They are quite beside themselves!

CAIAPHAS

Oh, Father Abraham! I am not deaf!

SERVANT

On their way here just now, it seems they, they saw the, the -

CAIAPHAS

Say it out, man!

SERVANT

Beyond our gates, High Priest! In the city streets! There are walking dead!

CAIAPHAS

What?!

SERVANT

The maids have seen it with their own eyes, Rabbi! Devout Jews, long since gone to their rest, are out of their graves and abroad in Jerusalem!..

CONSTERNATION...   DARKEN THE CONFERENCE ROOM.

SCENE TWENTY TWO

LIGHT AREA, FRONT STAGE.

AMON, AZOR, SADOC AND JORAM MOVE QUICKLY INTO
THE LIGHT AND "SPREAD OUT."
THEY STOP, SET DOWN THEIR BRIEF CASES, FOUR
ABREAST...
EACH PROCLAIMS IN TURN TO THE AUDIENCE:

AMON

Am I to believe my ears?! They are here among us - in Judaea, in
Jerusalem!

AZOR

They witness openly, preach boldly - in the streets, the squares, from
the very rooftops! -

SADOC

That Jesus, Jesus of Nazareth is, is - oh, I cannot bring myself to say
it! -

AMON

Blasphemy! And all who speak out thus and thus are vile
blasphemers! -

JORAM

Headless chickens? Well, no. Actually... They are open,
staunch, well-nigh valiant in their -

266

AZOR

'Driven to reckless exuberance! They are joyous, exultant - like men sated on wine!

SADOC

Converts! By the score - the hundredfold! Week after week -

JORAM

A new baptism, talk of a second dispensation, a final covenant! -

AMON

They repeat it again and again - a veritable mantra! -

JORAM

That he died in accord with the Scriptures, that he was buried, that he was raised again on the third day - all in fulfillment of the prophesies of yore!

SADOC

Mantra indeed! Repeated often enough, one comes to believe it! -

AZOR

Stupid, oh so stupid! Idiots! Gullible, dastardly morons! -

AMON

Tell them the moon is made of cheese and they will ask, can we have a piece!

AZOR

'Trot after the first carrot that is dangled before them! The oh, so very common, common people! -

SADOC

Of course, this so-called Resurrection is a myth! No eye-witnesses, none! No collaborative evidence - not as much as a shred of concrete proof! -

AMON

Nothing to go on but the hallucinations of two women, eye-straining in the fickle light of a dubious dawn! -

SADOC

And yet still they are being won over, gladly embracing the hearsay of the Magdalene, the so-called witness of fishermen, ignorati! -

JORAM

And nothing we say or do seems to stem the flow away from Orthodoxy! Now it is a veritable hemorrhage in the body of Judaism! -

AMON

Our very power-base is being eroded -

SADOC

Who ever heard of Gentile baptism? Unthinkable! And yet month after -

AZOR

And so the schism spreads, relentlessly! Samaria, Syria, Macedonia!

JORAM

And thence - who can tell? - to the Greek Isles!? -

AMON

And should this cult reach further still - to the heart of Empire, Rome? -

JORAM

Or if it reaches - as it needs must - Caesarea -

AZOR

Then the Procurator will know -

sedition is rife in the land he governs!

SADOC

And the question will be asked - where did this nonsense originate? -

JORAM

All eyes will turn on Jerusalem -

AZOR

Our Holy City will be scrutinised as never before -

SADOC

Its people, customs, traditions - buildings -

AZOR

Its seat of religious observance - the Temple -

AMON

Oh, Father Abraham! Our very Temple - in jeopardy!..

AZOR, AMON AND SADOC TURN, MOVE UPSTAGE,
EXEUNT.
JORAM MAKES TO FOLLOW, THEN TURNS BACK; SPOT ON
HIM. AGAIN DIRECT ADDRESS TO AUDIENCE.

JORAM

Yes, but how account for their gift of tongues?

Astonishing...

And how explain - oh, how explain! –

this instant reversal,

this sudden change in the Galileans –

from feckless to fearless?..

How, indeed?..

Unless... unless?..   FADE SPOT ON JORAM.

SCENE TWENTY THREE

LIGHT CONFERENCE ROOM TO REVEAL CAIPHAS SEATED
AT THE HEAD OF THE TABLE.
AMON, AZOR, JORAM AND SADOC ENTER, SIT, OPEN
BRIEF CASES... FUSS OVER PAPERS, MEMOS, ETC.

CAIAPHAS

So... Let us have your reports. Come, be brief. Sadoc?

SADOC

Eh-hh, there are rumours that -

CAIPHAS

Facts, Sadoc, facts! Spare me your rumours.

SADOC

Well... it seems that -

CAIPHAS

Seems? Seems!

SADOC

They, they have begun to say such and such about us, High Priest.

CAIPHAS

What? Say it out.

SADOC

That, that back there, at the Praetorium, when we demanded the
death penalty and Pilate washed his hands...

AZOR

We, we screamed with one voice -

'His blood be upon us - and upon our children.'

CAIAPHAS

What?!.. No!? -

AMON

'Going from mouth to mouth even as we speak -

JORAM

It is true, Rabbi. I have witnessed it with my own ears.

CAIAPHAS

But, but we never said such a - never occurred to us! Not our words - ever!.. Oh, great harm will come to the Jews because of this!..

AMON

Denigrating, demonising us! Putting words on our lips we never, ever -

CAIAPHAS

What a contemptible libel! What base person would spread such a - ?

SADOC

They say Levi. Once a tax collector. Now called Matthew.

AZOR

One of their leaders. And a dangerous one. In years to come, perchance, his witness may be set down, scribed -

AMON

Copied. Again and again. Passed on from one generation to the next.

SADOC

And the fools will believe it - swallow every last word!..

JORAM

Of course, we did not say so - not in so many words. But the sentiment -

CAIAPHAS

Sentiment? Sentiment!.. Look you, Rabbi Joram - we invoked the
Law, not a curse on our offspring!..

AMON

And what is more...

CAIAPHAS

More? What more?

AZOR

Somehow - somehow - the witness of the soldiers at the tomb -

CAIAPHAS

Reached him? This man, this Matthew? Has wind of it?

SADOC

But how? Our bribe was meant to seal their lips for evermore!

AMON

A leak, hint - who knows? A tongue loosed by wine and high living -

CAIAPHAS

And they know?

AZOR

Be assured - and are using it as a trump card, a pawn whereby to
promote their cause...

SADOC

Oh, Father Abraham! We are undone! -

CAIAPHAS

Not so! Oh, not so! While I live - and to my last breath - I will
defend Jewry, assert the Orthodoxy of our one, true religion! Mark
my words: the God of Abraham, Isaac and Jacob will come to our
aid! Ours is far from a lost cause!...   FADE.

SCENE TWENTY FOUR

LIGHT THE PC AREA.

ENTER AMON.
HE CROSSES, PASSES THE COMPUTER,
CHECKS, TURNS BACK, SURVEYS THE SCREEN...

THEN HE SITS AT THE DESK, BEGINS TO TAP VARIOUS
KEYS.
HE REACHES FOR PAPER AND PEN, BEGINS TO MAKE
NOTES.

DARKEN THE PC AREA.

SCENE TWENTY SIX

LIGHT THE CONFERENCE ROOM. CAIAPHAS SEATED AT
THE TOP OF THE TABLE. AZOR AND SADOC ENTER, SEAT
THEMSELVES...

CAIAPHAS

So... how say you now?

SADOC

And still the cancer grows apace, High Priest -

AZOR

They speak of him as if he were alive - more alive than when he
lived -

SADOC

'Call him Saviour, Redeemer -

CAIAPAS

A Messiah, huh! A Messiah from Galilee! Back from the dead, no
less!

AZOR

Not simply Messiah, Caiaphas -

CAIAPHAS

What?

AZOR

They have begun to address him as, as...

CAIAPHAS

Speak. Say it out.

AZOR

Master. Lord and Master.

CAIAPHAS

What?!.. But, but that is a title reserved for Emperors – for the Most High!

AZOR

Indeed. And they know it.

SADOC

Their choice of title is deliberate... calculated.

CAIAPHAS

Calculated to drive me into a frenzy!.. Is this what you tell me - they look on this Jesus as, as akin to God?!

AZOR

Son of God...

CAIAPHAS

So, wonder of wonders, God has a son!

A son who spent his life with sinners and publicans,

died on an ignominious cross between two thieves!

But then God - our magnanimous, omniscient God -

raised him from the dead, freed him from the tomb,

so that we can all exult in his splendiferous glory!

Oh, come, come, my colleagues! Insult my intelligence no further!..

CAIAPHAS SEARCHES THROUGH PAPERS, FINDS A DOCUMENT.

This, this Jesus - had he a father, a mother?.. Yes, yes we know so!

'Marked well his progeny long since. Sired by one, Joseph, a

carpenter. 'Born of eh, eh... (CONSULTING DOCUMENT) one,

Mary. Why, no more common a female name in all Judaea!

Son of God? Offspring of Nazarenes!.. Oh, the blasphemy of it! The

arrogance! The sheer, unadulterated onslaught on our most cherished

beliefs!..

Of all the world's religions, only one - Judaism -

has been, is now, always will be, monotheistic!

One God. One only God. One true God.

And that belief we will defend to our dying breath!..

MURMURING ASSENT.

So... Let us have done with the absurd, return to reality... Oh. Why,

pray, do we not have a full quorum? Where is Amon?

AZOR

Delayed, perhaps. I glimpsed him on the corridor within the hour.

SADOC

He will be here anon. You may be sure of it, High Priest.

CAIAPHAS

And Joram? What of Joram?   (UNEASE. HESITANT)

Well?..

AZOR

Why, I have not laid eyes on him these past few days.

SADOC

Nor I, High Priest...

CAIAPHAS

Oh-hh? Ill, perhaps?..

AZOR

Or ill disposed...

CAIAPHAS

Huh. Do, do you tell me that a member of our Inner Circle - a fellow of this most secret Conclave - has absconded, yielded to obnoxious schism, gone in search of a myth?..

AZOR

It, it would seem so, yes...

CAIPHAS

But, but that cannot, must not, be so!

ENTER AMON IN HASTE, BREATHLESS... JOINS THEM,

AMON

Apologies, High Priest. I assure you I -

CAIAPHAS

Yes, yes, Amon!.. You have notes?

AMON

Alas, yes. To do with Rabbi Joram -

CAIAPHAS

What?

AMON

He has been scrolling -

CAIAPHAS

Again? But I strictly forbade him to -

AMON

'Left the computer on, so urgent was his need to, to leave...

CAIAPHAS

Hmmm... You have been to his abode?

AMON   (NODDING)

Empty. Intact. Apart from his - necessities...

CAIAPHAS

I see... So... What pearls of wisdom has he uncovered this time?
Enough, doubtless, to explain his sudden, secretive departure from
righteousness?..

AMON READS ALOUD, BREAKING THE SENTENCES:

Zechariah... Eleven, thirteen:
And they weighed out my wages - thirty shekels of silver.
But Yahweh told me, 'Throw it into the Treasury,
this princely sum at which they have valued me.'
Taking the thirty shekels of silver, I threw them into
the Temple of Yahweh, into the Treasury...

UNEASE... MURMURING.

CAIAPHAS

What? Is this Joram's last word - that we, in our collective wisdom,
were but pawns in a pre-ordained scheme - ?!

278

AZOR

Pre-ordained by the Most High himself? From the beginning of - ?

AZOR

Thirty shekels of - !

SADOC

There is no denying Deuteronomy - *One who has been hanged is accursed of God!*

AZOR

The very Pentateuch! As against the ambiguous screed of a minor prophet!

CAIAPHAS GETS TO HIS FEET. HE IS OLDER, NOW... STOOPED.

CAIAPHAS

So... It has come to this. Treachery most vile.

SADOC

What he will not disclose! -

AZOR

'Reveal our machinations - to protect ourselves, defend the Covenant!

SADOC

'Twill out. Even as we speak -

AZOR

No doubt... 'Never liked him, Joram. 'Never could take to him -

SADOC

'Something about him. His waywardness -

AZOR

'Querying. 'Asking all those questions -

SADOC

A disruptive nuisance! 'Would never do what he was told! Well,

good riddance, that's what I say!..

CAIPHAS

Is there - more?..

AMON

Only a note in his own hand...

CAIAPHAS

Read it.

AMON

Eh, I think, perhaps, High Priest -

CAIAPHAS

Aloud.

AMON

As you wish...   (READING)

"It is possible to read a prophesy, again and again, and still not see it

- until it is fulfilled..."

SADOC

What rubbish! -

AZOR

How pretentious of him to - !

AMON

Still, there are similarities, doubtless...

CAIAPHAS

What?

AMON

Why, between the words of the prophet and what took place under this very roof -

SADOC :

Superficial! All of it superfic -

CAIAPHAS

Oh, Amon, Amon! Will you, too, follow in the defector's footsteps?

AMON

Why, no, High Priest! I was merely pointing out that indeed -

CAIAPHAS

Had Joram listened to my admonitions, heeded my warnings, obeyed my wishes, he would still be with us this day - and not an outcast we know not where! Nor would dissension have raised its ugly head among us!..

SADOC

A split! A veritable rupture! -

AZOR

Unless we are one we are nothing! -

SADOC

Then heed our High Priest, Amon, heed him well! -

CAIPHAS

Scroll the Scriptures as you will there is no denying the testimony of eye-witnesses in our own time, the evidence of what we ourselves have seen and heard...

ASSENT... AGREEMENT.

And for this he has left us?.. Because of a dubious snatch here, a doubtful sentence there, he has abandoned his vocation, scorned my authority, deserted his people - men and women who held him in high esteem?..

Oh, you fool, Joram!.. You idiot!..

And how dangerous it is to be a dreamer of dreams abroad in this land...

CAIAPHAS SLUMPS BACK IN HIS CHAIR...

And who else among you will defect - now that he has made his exit, shown the way?..

SADOC

Not I -

AZOR

Nor I -

AMON

You may be sure of our enduring allegiance, Chief Rabbi...

CAIPHAS

Hmmm... But convinced or no?.. Convinced utterly?.. Or could it be that you are afraid to make a move - for fear of insecurity?.. 'Reluctant to sever the status quo, step into the unknown?..

What?!.. Am I to be serviced by parasites, surrounded by yes-men even as I enter old age?! Do!.. Do as you so believe!.. In your innermost selves... But not to please this ageing High Priest!.. Not to placate me! I will have no fawning in my Sanhedrin!

And if, tomorrow, there are further vacant seats at my Conference table, then so be it... I would not have it otherwise. Oh, spare me a Rabbi saying one thing, thinking - believing - another!..

I am too old to change, now. Nor do I wish to... Were I to live to four score and ten I could never, ever, accept, come to believe in, this Jesus of Nazareth...

DARKEN THE CONFERENCE ROOM.

SCENE TWENTY SIX

LIGHT THE CONFERENCE ROOM. CAIAPHAS, AMON, AZOR AND SADOC HAVE NOW AGED. CAIAPHAS SLUMPED AT TABLE.

SADOC

What to do, what to do?..

AMON

What?

SADOC

How stem this tide of schism before we are all engulfed?

AMON

Oh-hh... Would that we had ten such as Saul.

AZOR

Rabbi Saul? Indeed! If ever there was a defender of the one, true religion!

AMON

A Pharisee and the son of a Pharisee! -

SADOC

No more learned scribe in all Jewry -

AZOR

A profound Doctor of the Law -

SADOC

Valiant defender of our most cherished traditions -

AZOR

'Young man - a wondrous career ahead of him -

AMON

'Spares himself nothing in persecuting the enemy -

AZOR

Why, they are in abject fear of him, so ferocious are his tactics -

AMON

'Small wonder that they quake at the very mention of his name -

AZOR

Even as we speak he is on the road to Damascus -

SADOC :

Once there, he will hound the dissidents, relentlessly -

AMON

Unless... unless -

AZOR

What?

AMON

Oh, 'tis nothing! But a vain fancy –

CAIAPHAS ROUSES HIMSELF, LOOKS UP.

CAIAPHAS

Come, Amon. Say it out.

AMON

Well... eh, what if he is won over by, by their counter-arguments?..

MURMURING... AGITATION.

SADOC

What!

AZOR

Saul? Saul of Tarsus?

SADOC

Con-converted?

AZOR

Our Saul? Rabbi Saul?..

SADOC

'Go, go over to them?..

CAIAPHAS

Saul?.. Saul of - Tarsus?.. 'Become a, a Christian?..

HE BEGINS TO CHUCKLE... THE OTHERS JOIN IN...
TENTATIVELY, AT FIRST, NERVOUSLY... THEN BEGIN
TO LAUGH, OUTRIGHT.
A LAUGHTER THAT GRADUALLY INCREASES IN
VOLUME...

THE END

The baptism of Jesus in the Jordan.

One member of the Sanhedrin, a Pharisee called Gamaliel,

who was a doctor of the Law

and respected by the whole people

stood up and addressed the Sanhedrin:

If this enterprise, this movement of theirs, is of
human origin it will break up of its own accord;
but if it does in fact come from God
you will not only be unable to destroy them,
but you might find yourself fighting against God.

- ACTS 5: 34-39.

SEAN WALSH

Has lived and worked in communications all his life:
journalist, subeditor, editor, director/producer,
actor, preacher, script writer – in Ireland and abroad.
Former Head of Drama, Radio, RTE.

His scripts have been broadcast on RTE, Radio One,
BBC 4 and, in translation, on European networks;
televised on RTE One, BBC One and Channel 4;
staged at the Peacock by the Abbey National Theatre,
at the Project, the Liverpool Playhouse
and on the London Fringe…

Credits include:
The Night of the Rouser.   Earwig.
The Dreamers. Fugitive. Veil.
Penny for Your Travels. Far Side of the Moon.
Three for Calvary. Pilate Under Pressure.
Jenny One, Two, Three…
The Circus. Centre Circle. Gluepot.
Where Do We Go from Here, My Lovely?
At The Praetorium.   Conclave.
Assault on a Citadel.

Also on Amazon: Notes on the Past Imperfect. At the Praetorium.
Veil. Pilate Under Pressure etc. (paperback and Kindle)

Has facilitated many workshops on Creative/Script Writing
in Dublin and at various centres around Ireland.

Major new work: THE RECKONING. In two acts/parts.
In search of a home/director/producer. Theatre? Cinema?

Website: www.sean-walsh.me

THE WRITER MEETS THE PRESS

ON THE NIGHT OF March 27, 2013, at All Hollows, Dublin 9, the curtain came down on the third and last performance of *At the Praetorium*. (Last but hopefully not final!) A play that has since happily morphed into *Pilate Under Pressure...*

Later - much later! - Sean Walsh reluctantly agreed to a Press Conference. (He is quite shy, really, hates beating his own drum - in case you hadn't noticed...)

So there he was, on the rostrum, mineral water to hand, seated before an array of microphones, taking questions from the floor…

Q: (Wexford People)
Were you surprised at the turnout?

SEAN:
Gobsmacked. I mean, the weather was cat that evening. Snow, sleet, freezing. I began to wonder, who in their right minds would venture out on such a night? As we used to say in another age,"You wouldn't put out a milk bottle…"

Q: (Limerick Leader)
Yet you had a full house?

SEAN:
Near enough. 200+! I couldn't believe it! And what an audience! You could hear a pin drop! And then as the lights went down on the final scene, applause! Applause! No holding back!
Increasing in volume as the cast came back on to take a well-deserved bow…

Q: (National Catholic Reporter)
You will have noticed that the applause increased in volume even further when you were called upon to say a final few words?

SEAN:
I was hoping you wouldn't mention that... Yes, it did, didn't it?.. Their way of saying, I suppose, they had never witnessed a play quite like it until now... then.

Q: (The Skibereen Eagle)
You would describe your piece as a Passion play - with a difference?

Sean:
I dislike the term, I really do. It conjures up holy women, flying angels, celestial shepherds. I have absolutely no interest in writing a morality play in the traditional mould. I set myself the task of writing about ordinary human beings on the horns of a dilemma. Caught in crisis. Having to make a decision. Nothing black and white about it. It is almost - if not quite - incidental that the piece is set against the backdrop of the first Good Friday.

Q: (Der Spiegel)
Obviously, your drama did not come to you out of the blue? Can you trace its growth?

SEAN:
Back in the 50's when I was a student in Rome, our student master, Father Alexander Kerrigan O F M, a Scripture scholar of no small repute, gave a talk/lecture to the students: The Passion according to Matthew. *I listened, spellbound. Ideas, slants, insights... with a strong leaning towards German research.*

I managed somehow - don't ask me how, I can't remember - to get my hands on the typescript when the lecture ended. A keeper? I'll say! I have it to this day, safely in a filing cabinet, pages yellowed with age.

It was to this MSS I would turn, decades later, when I began to put pen to paper, write the drama that would become, eventually, At the Praetorium.

The idea really began to germinate back in the sixties when I was a visitor in the Big Apple. I found Greenwich Village - as it was then - quite fascinating. There I saw Theatre-in-the-Round for the very first time - I was amazed...

Then one evening I went to a cinema quite off Broadway to see a film, **The Gospel According to Matthew,** *directed by a young, relatively unknown Italian,* **Pier Paulo Pasolini.**

In black and white. Stark, barren landscapes. A cast of extras, no big names, no stars. So different from the Hollywood treatment of the Christ story. I was blown away...

I emerged from that cinema into a humid New York night. And the thought came to me - why not the Passion according to Matthew? That was the start of a long road.

Q: (The Scottish Sunday Post)

You're talking fifty years ago, and more. This has to be the longest germination in history!

SEAN:
Well, I was doing other things, had to. But I kept coming back to what I sensed was a rich idea - reading, researching, taking notes, asking questions, sketching outlines, scenes...

Then, a few years ago, I met and became friendly with Father Martin Hogan, a lecturer in Sacred Scripture at Mater Dei, Dublin City University. (He was chaplain in my own parish of Corpus Christi, Drumcondra, D 9) He became my mentor, came to my rescue again and again when I got bogged down in exegesis.

And when he asked me to write a short play that could be done in our church, I produced a piece about Pilate, his wife, her servant, a centurion - in which the central character does not appear but is constantly referred to...

Q: (IL Tempo)
But no prisoners?

SEAN:
*They were lurking in the wings! Let me explain: back in the 80's I
wrote and directed a drama for radio, Three for Calvary. It was
broadcast on RTE Radio One. The late Eamon Keane as Barabbas.*

*Three prisoners in a cell in the dungeons beneath the Praetorium,
the Roman fortress in Jerusalem, symbol of colonial power and
conquest... Who were they? What were they? How did they spend
their last night on earth? I had to get in there, sense their despair,
smell their sweat, taste their tears, share their confinement...*

*Ending with the release of Barabbas, leaving him in a daze, centre
stage, alone with the Roman officer:*

> Where will you go?
> Go?.. Why to Golgotha. I want to be close to Dismas and
> Gestas when it... gets darker and darker.
> You'll be near the crosses, I'll see to it.
> Besides, I... I want to look on the man who goes up in my
> place...

*Just last March it began to dawn on me: marry the two plays - a
kind of upstairs, downstairs scenario - and you have yourself an
hour-long Drama! Try, at least try... So I did. The result you saw
for yourselves - works very well, I reckon...*

Q: (The Guardian)
**Was that the complete chain, then, or was there still a link
missing?**

SEAN:
*The original version ended with Pilate's sudden dismissal of Joseph
of Arimathea:*

> Enough! You vex me further at your peril! Now go -
> see to this, this cadaver. I rule the living - not the
> dead!..

Crescendo, yes. But more than a whit abruptly. The audience was thrown, they needed more, wanted a smoother landing... I began to mull, as is my wont...

In June, a few years ago, my wife and I visited Paris. I wanted to view the Rembrant *exhibition in the Louvre:* Rembrant et la figure du Christ.

I was fascinated by the various sketches the Master made as he tried one thing, then another, searching for a real-life portrait of Jesus. (These were mounted on the walls of the exhibition area.)

Fascinated, too, by his modus agendi: it seems he recruited one Jew after another from among the local population in his home town, had them back to his apartment, sit for him while he sketched...

And so to the original, the finished work, a portrait of Christ like no other before... A true original that spurned the unreal images of the Middle Ages and the Renaissance... I could only stand in awe and wonderment.

No, let me finish! The next morning I rose early, sat at the table by the window, reached for paper and pen... That exhibition had triggered something in me and within the hour I had completed the first draft of what was to become - several drafts later - the final scene:

Pilate rises, turns to his officer, incredulous –

> Do I hear you aright? They want me to send soldiers under my command to guard a tomb? A tomb!? Why, I would be the laughing stock of the Empire!.. Go tell them, the Governor of Judaea will not be privy to this folly!..
>
> Eh-hh... They have guards of their own, have they not, mercenaries in their pay? Well, then, let them see to it.

Q: (The Limerick Leader)

Which brings me neatly to my question: the style of writing differs each time the storyline moves upstairs. Is this deliberate?

SEAN:
I would say so, yes. The scenes in the cell: ordinary, everyday dialogue. Upstairs, the dialogue goes up a notch or two. More stylised, a greater emphasis on assonance and alliteration. Without appearing contrived, hopefully...

And with a respectful nod towards Ben Hur *and* A Man for All Seasons - *to mention but two sources of inspiration... One more question and I'll have to call it a day, I'm very tired...*

Q: (Le Figaro)
Do you plan another drama along the same lines?

SEAN:
No. I move on from here. Quod scripsi, scripsi... That's it. But I do have in mind to publish all three plays as a single paperback. Holding title: **Good Friday Revisited...**

Starting with **At the Praetorium/Pilate Under Pressure**... *The Roman perspective/dilemma...*

Then **Veil***: depicting a Jewish family in Jerusalem and how the Passion impacts on their lives...*

Ending with **Conclave.** *Behind closed doors. Inside the Sanhedrin.*

That's about it. 'Should make quite a trilogy, don't you think?..

On trial at Jerusalem:
Jesus of Nazareth - or the Governor of Judaea?..

PILATE
UNDER PRESSURE

SEAN WALSH

What! A choice between the Emperor of Rome and the King of the Jews?
Don't be absurd! The decision was obvious - no contention!..

HEANEY ON VEIL

Department of English, Queen's University, Belfast.   1966.

VEIL by Sean Walsh

The idea of approaching the significance of the Passion obliquely, through the experiences of those who might be regarded as enemies, is good theatre; and the actual denouement is all the more dramatic for not taking place in the presence of the Saviour.

In fact, the reality of the Incarnation seems to me properly realised in the movement - Christ's life becomes dynamic and efficacious in the world...

The devil's part, as ever in literature, comes off best here, I think...

Sadoc is a very consistent and interesting character whose psychology, though not as inherently interesting as Azarias's, is made concrete in his machinations.

Azarias is a rounded character whose development is at once true and inevitable: we watch a man finding some kind of grace in spite of himself, reaching fulfilment as much through circumstances as through personality - who sees the light in spite of himself, as it were.

Ruth, Veronica and Benjamin are all right as straight characters...

In the main, the speech is attractively dignified and in character.

And I think that Misach's outbreak in the end is the most exciting thing in the play, both as a dramatic device and as speech - after long silence.

Misach, incidentally, would be my nominee for the best dramatic figure in the cast.

Definitely a step well beyond the weeping women and the cowering apostles. I was kept reading, which is the most important thing in the end...

- Seamus Heaney.

(I knew very little about Seamus Heaney back then - and he knew nothing about me!..)

NOTES ON THE PAST IMPERFECT

Moves forward and backwards - sometimes sideways! Disjointed narrative - rather than neatly strung together...

The text: sometimes prose... other times, poetic prose... ever so often, poetry - in free style...

Hard to define, my book - literary fiction, a kind of memoir, more than somewhat autobiographical... A mosaic of sorts. Spiced with a wry sense of humour.

Writing "within myself"- for sure...
'Will make you forget you are reading a book?.. Again, for sure.
I avoid the traditional narrative format for the most part; I prefer direct speech - monologue, dialogue. (I've left out the bits the readers would skip, anyway!)

To begin to read... then find yourself listening... to a voice, voices... from another place, another time... Voices from Ireland of the 80's... Phone calls, recalls, spilt milk... The pain and the laughter, sorrow and joy, of a Yesterday world.

If your need is to be spoon-fed, if you have little desire to be challenged, mentally stimulated, if you wish to be left untouched in your comfort zone, if you have no stomach for the fray... then this is not the book for you!

It is me talking/ confessing to my fellow man. And if my words strike a note in the heart of Everyman, that is reward enough – to know that, deep down, I have made contact with Mankind…

A former colleague of mine in RTE, John Quinn, an educationalist, public speaker and himself a writer of no small stature wrote me:

Dear Sean,
I have been reading "Notes on the Past Imperfect."
Heart-wrenching to read, assuredly difficult to write, but you fashioned an extraordinary story from that imperfect past with great courage and honesty. An amazing achievement to forge a unity from the six stories and to do it while remaining true to the monologue /dialogue format with such consistency. Well done!

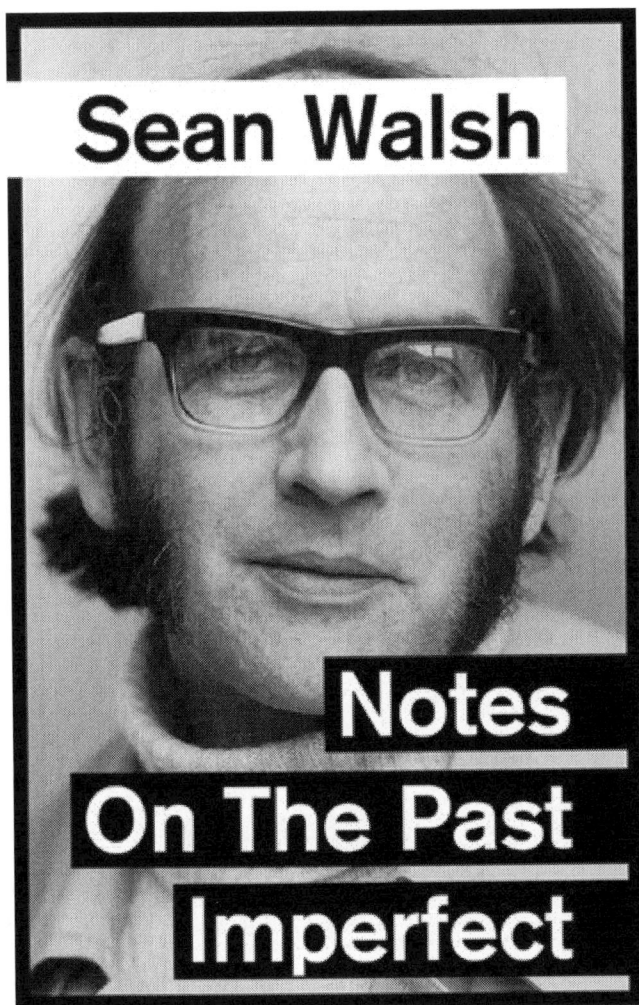

Sean Walsh
Notes On The Past Imperfect

"Penny for Your Travels" particularly moving and beautifully told.

Brilliant title!

So thank you and congratulations.

Be proud.

John.

Wee letter from Yesteryear.

(I will treasure it – for always.)

28.5.'14. A letter I received in the post touched me deeply. I share some lines from it – but not the name or identity of the writer.

"Dear Sean,

I'm asking myself how do I write this letter to a man who is so gifted with words. Anyway, here I go… Your book, Notes on the Past Imperfect, spoke right to my heart. I cried a lot reading it but also smiled at parts.

The one thing that came across powerfully to me was your deep love for Jenny and her love for you – it touched me to the core of my being. I love the words you often spoke to her – "A leanna…" Beautiful.

You have a deep understanding of matters of the heart. Page 80 in your book: "Trouble is, Padre, I find it well-nigh impossible to forgive – me…"

Thank you from my heart for your truth and honesty written in these precious pages. You have helped me on my own journey. I'm not very good at expressing myself, just want you to know how grateful I am.

God bless you always…"

PENNY FOR YOUR TRAVELS

Eighty years agrowing – and still growing...

SEAN WALSH

Chain still coming out of muddy water – a link at a time...

"*First and foremost write the book you want to write, not the one you – or others – think will sell. Write with a fire in your heart and you'll create something special, something readers will want to read. There may be all sorts of received wisdom out there about 'what agents are looking for' or 'what publishers want' or 'what's selling' but who wants a second-rate copy of someone else's idea?*" – Jane Johnson. Editor. Harpur Collins.